Cambridge
checl

NEW EDITION

checkpoint
English

2

John Reynolds

Cambridge
checkpoint

Endorsed by
**University of Cambridge
International Examinations**

NEW EDITION

checkpoint
English

2

HODDER
EDUCATION
AN HACHETTE UK COMPANY

Acknowledgements

The publishers would like to thank the following for permission to reproduce copyright material:

Text credits

pp.1–3 Yuri Nagibin, from 'The Winter Oak' from *Opening Worlds: Short Stories from Different Cultures* (Heinemann Educational, 2002); **pp.4–6** H.G. Wells, from *The Time Machine* (1895), reproduced by permission of A.P. Watt Ltd on behalf of The Literary Executors of the Estate of H.G. Wells; **pp.7–8** Mary Chiappe, from *Cabbages and Kings* (HKB Press, 2006), reproduced by permission of the author; **p.10** Bill Bryson, from *Neither Here Nor There* (Black Swan, 1998), reproduced by permission of The Random House Group Ltd; **pp.11–13** Edgar Allan Poe, from 'The Fall of the House of Usher' (1839); **pp.18–19** Samuel Pepys, from *Samuel Pepys's Diary* (1825); **pp.20–1** Anne Frank, from *The Diary of a Young Girl* (Puffin Books, 2007), reproduced by permission of Anne Frank Fonds; **p.23** A.L. Hendriks, 'Road to Lacovia' from *Talk of the Tamarinds*, edited by A. Forde (Hodder Education, 1971); **pp.26–7** George and Weedon Grossmith, from *The Diary of a Nobody* (1892); **pp.30–1** 'Legends of Langkawi', website text from *www.neosentuban.com.my*, reproduced by permission of Neo Sentuhan Sdn Bhd; **pp.32–3** Karen Carr, 'Theseus and the Minotaur', website text from *www.historyforkids.org/learn/greeks/religion/myths/theseus2.htm*, adapted and reproduced by permission of Kidipede; **p.34** 'The Beast of Bodmin', online tourist guide from *www.cornwalls.co.uk/myths-legends/beast_of_bodmin.htm*; **pp.35–6** Hillary Mayell, 'Bermuda Triangle: Behind the intrigue', online article from *http://news.nationalgeographic.com/news/2002/12/1205_021205_bermudatriangle_2.htm*, reproduced by permission of National Geographic Stock; **pp.37–9** 'Rama and Sita' from *http://naturenest.wordpress.com/2008/11/04/the-story-of-rama-sita-a-tale-for-diwali*; **pp.44–6** 'Rocky Springs Park' leaflet from *http://www.themeparkbrochures.net/197x1.html*; **pp.48–9** 'Got a teenager?', Parentline Plus leaflet from *www.gotateenager.org.uk/files/pdf/gotateenager.pfd*, reproduced by permission of Family Lives; **pp.50–1** 'Death Valley Eggs' leaflet from *http://www.animalaid.co.uk/images/pdf/eggleaflet.pdf*, reproduced by permission of Animal Aid; **pp.57–9** William Shakespeare, from *Romeo and Juliet* (1623); **pp.60–2** Ruth Prawer Jhabvala, from 'The Young Couple' in *A Stronger Climate* (John Murray, 1968), reproduced by permission of Maia Publishing Services Ltd; **pp.65–6** James Meikle and Adam Gabbatt, 'Airports closed as volcanic ash drifts towards UK' from *Guardian* Online (17 April, 2010), copyright Guardian News & Media Ltd 2010, reproduced by permission of the publisher; **pp.67–9** Neil Syson and Carl Stroud, from 'Ash wreaks havoc across Europe' from *The Sun* (17 April 2010), copyright © 2010, reproduced by permission of News International Syndication; **pp.71–2** Laura Redpath, 'Jamaican sprinter Lerone Clarke strikes gold at Commonwealth Games' from *Daily Gleaner* (8 October 2010), reproduced by permission of The Gleaner Company Limited; **pp.73–4** 'Magnificent Pandelela' from *New Strait Times of Malaysia* (12 October 2010); **p.77** William Howard Russell, from article in the London *Times* (November 1854); **pp.78–9** Alfred Tennyson, 'The Charge of the Light Brigade' (1854); **pp.80–2** Quentin Letts, 'Why I hate squirrels!' from *Daily Mail* (21 July, 2010), reproduced by permission of Solo Syndication; **p.84** Alex Zane, 'Lightyears Ahead' – review of film 'Toy Story 3' from *www.thesun.co.uk/sol/homepage/showbiz/film/3056447/Alex-Zane-Toy-Story-3-is-lightyears-ahead.html*, reproduced by permission of News International Syndication; **p.85** Peter Travers – review of 'Toy Story 3' from *www.rollingstone.com/movies/reviews/toy-story-3-2010061*; **p.86** Armond White, from review of 'Toy Story 3' from *www.nypress.com/article-21357-bored-game.html*; **pp.88–9** Keith Waterhouse, from 'The eggcup that does it all sideways' from *Daily Mail* (8 May 2008), reproduced by permission of Solo Syndication; **pp.92–5** Charles Dickens, from *Hard Times* (1854); **pp.98–100** Vuk Pavlovic, 'The wickedest city' from *http://www.thewayofthepirates.com/history-of-piracy/port-royal.php*, reproduced by permission of the author; **pp.100–101** Bill Bryson, from *The Life and Times of the Thunderbolt Kid* (Black Swan, 1997), reproduced by permission of The Random House Group Ltd; **pp.101–103** Anna Rockall, from 'Christmas Island' from *http://www.guardian.co.uk/travel/2001/dec/22/wildlifeholidays.christmasisland.guardiansaturdaytravelsection* (22 December 2001), copyright Guardian News & Media Ltd 2001, reproduced by permission of the publisher; **pp.104–106** Lonely Planet review and Traveller's review for Bako National Park from *http://www.lonelyplanet.com/malaysia/malaysian-borneo-sarawak/bako-national-park/sights/nature/bako-national-park/sights/nature/bako-national-park*, reproduced by permission of Lonely Planet Publications Pty Ltd; **p.107** Edith Wharton, from *A Backward Glance* (1934); **pp.116–7** from *Beowulf*; **pp.118–9** from *Sir Gawain and the Green Knight*; **p.120** Geoffrey Chaucer, 'The Miller' from *The Canterbury Tales*.

All designated trademarks and brands are protected by their respective trademarks.

Photo credits

p.2 © Christian Delbert – Fotolia; **p.11** © The Granger Collection, NYC/TopFoto; **p.20** The Diary of a Young Girl: The Definitive Edition by Anne Frank, edited by Otto H Frank and Mirjam Pressler, translated by Susan Massotty (Viking 1997, Puffin Books 1997, Puffin Modern Classics 2001, 2007) copyright © The Anne Frank-Fonds, Basle, Switzerland, 1991. English translation copyright © Doubleday a division of Bantam Doubleday Dell Publishing Group Inc, 1995. ISBN 978014131519. Reproduced by Permission of Penguin Books Ltd; **p.30** © Eye Ubiquitous/CORBIS; **p.32** © The Art Gallery Collection/Alamy; **p.34** *t* © Dale Crook/Alamy, *c* © Times Newspapers/Rex Features, *b* © David Beauchamp/Rex Features; **p.39** © AJAY VERMA/Reuters/Corbis; **p.65** © ARNI SAEBERG/AFP/Getty Images; **p.67** *t* © NASA/MODIS Rapid Response Team, *b* © John McLellan/Rex Features; **p.68** *l* © Geoffrey Robinson/Rex Features, *r* © Sipa Press/Rex Features; **p.69** © Ben Stansall/AFP/Getty Images; **p.71** © Michael Steele/Getty Images; **p.73** © Matt King/Getty Images; **p.80** © tina7si – Fotolia; **p.82** © NEPENTHE PRODUCTIONS/Ronald Grant Archive; **p.84** © BuenaVist/Everett/Rex Features; **p.85** © BuenaVist/Everett/Rex Features; **p.102** © Jurgen Freund/Nature Picture Library/Rex Features; **p.105** © pwollinga – Fotolia

t = top, *c* = centre, *b* = bottom, *l* = left, *r* = right

Every effort has been made to trace all copyright holders, but if any have been inadvertently overlooked the publishers will be pleased to make the necessary arrangements at the first opportunity.

Hachette UK's policy is to use papers that are natural, renewable and recyclable products and made from wood grown in sustainable forests. The logging and manufacturing processes are expected to conform to the environmental regulations of the country of origin.

Orders: please contact Bookpoint Ltd, 130 Milton Park, Abingdon, Oxon OX14 4SB. Telephone: (44) 01235 827720. Fax: (44) 01235 400454. Lines are open 9.00–5.00, Monday to Saturday, with a 24-hour message answering service. Visit our website at www.hoddereducation.com.

© John Reynolds 2011
First published in 2011 by
Hodder Education, an Hachette UK Company,
338 Euston Road
London NW1 3BH

Impression number 5 4 3 2 1
Year 2015 2014 2013 2012 2011

Cover photo © Daryl Benson/Photographer's Choice/Getty Images
Illustrations by Oxford Designers and Illustrators
Typeset in Garamond Light 12pt by DC Graphic Design Limited, Swanley Village, Kent
Printed in Italy

A catalogue record for this title is available from the British Library
ISBN 978 1444 143850

Contents

CONTENTS

Introduction

Welcome to *Cambridge Checkpoint English Student's Book 2*. This is the second of a series of three books aimed at international students in stages 7–9 who are preparing for the Cambridge Checkpoint Tests, with a view to IGCSE and beyond. This is an integrated series of books (each with an accompanying teacher's resource book), offering a varied and challenging range of English experiences and assignments. The books provide a comprehensive introduction to the skills needed to succeed in English at this stage and can be used as a main teaching resource or to complement teachers' own schemes of work and other materials.

Covering curriculum requirements

The content of *Student's Book 2* is firmly rooted in the Cambridge Secondary 1 English Curriculum Framework for stage 8 and focuses on the key areas of reading and writing along with underlying emphasis on language study, grammatical usage and punctuation. These skills are consolidated and revisited through each book in the series. Each chapter also contains suggested speaking and listening activities.

In each chapter there is a thematic link between the reading and writing sections, and the stimulus material reflects the suggestions for reading in the Cambridge framework. The stimulus material is drawn from both fiction and non-fiction texts written in English from countries throughout the world and from different periods of time. Pre-twentieth century literature is amply represented and, wherever possible, in an unabridged format. Reading exercises test straightforward fact retrieval, understanding of vocabulary and inferential and interpretative reading skills. Writing tasks allow students to write in a variety of genres (related to the different stimulus material) and provide opportunities to write both short passages and more extended, complex responses, in some cases as part of a small group project.

Structure

Each of the three books comprising the *Checkpoint English* series is supported by a teacher's resource book which contains additional reference information, an audio CD and further suggestions for practice exercises related to each unit in the student's book. A number of pages in the teacher's resource books have been designed for photocopying and use in the classroom.

Each book in the series is divided into eight chapters and follows a similar pattern, beginning with exemplar reading passages illustrating a particular type or genre of writing, followed by exercises to test both understanding and appreciation of what has been read. A range of writing tasks is set, usually linked to the type of writing exemplified by the reading passages; there are also suggested speaking and listening activities and, in most chapters, some prose passages or poems intended for general reading interest. Each chapter also contains information on different key skills (punctuation, parts of speech and their functions, vocabulary building and spelling, etc.) and exercises to reinforce these. The final chapter in each book of the series follows a slightly different format from the other seven as it introduces pupils to a more general area of English study. Although the chapters in each book have been planned so that teachers can work through them progressively in chronological order if they wish, it is not an absolute requirement to approach the course in this way. The books allow for a flexible approach to teaching and the chapters can be taught in whatever order best fits with a teacher's own scheme of work.

Assessment

As mentioned in the previous section, each chapter contains a range of exercises which allow the assessment of students' progression through the various English skills required for success at this level. *Student's Book 3* includes a chapter containing exercises aimed at providing specific preparation for the Cambridge Checkpoint Tests although the assessment tasks which students complete throughout the different chapters also provide cumulatively a comprehensive preparation for these tests.

1 Descriptive writing to create an atmosphere and setting

Reading

In *Student's Book 1* we looked at ways in which writers describe characters and settings. Another important feature of imaginative writing is how the description of the setting or background to the story can create an atmosphere in the minds of readers that reinforces and underlines the story's main themes and topics.

Here is an extract from a short story by a Russian author, Yuri Nagibin, who tells how a young schoolteacher, Anna Vasilevna, learns an important lesson about the natural world from Savushkin, a student from the country of whom she has previously had a low opinion. Read the passage carefully and then answer the questions that follow on pages 3–4.

Extract 1: 'The Winter Oak'

The path along which Savushkin led Anna Vasilevna began just behind the school building. As soon as they stepped into the forest and the fir branches that looked like paws heavily laden with snow closed behind them, they were immediately transported into another world, an enchanted world of peace and silence. Magpies and crows flew from tree to tree, shaking the branches, knocking off the fir cones, and sometimes their wings caught on the dry, brittle twigs, and broke them. Yet not a sound could be heard.

All around everything was white. Only high up the wind had blown on the tops of the soaring weeping birches, so that they showed up black, and their delicate little branches looked as if they had been etched in Indian ink on the blue surface of the sky.

The path ran by the stream, sometimes alongside it, submissively following its twisting course, sometimes rising high up and winding along a steep bank.

Now and again the trees would part and reveal sunny, joyful glades, criss-crossed with hare tracks that looked like watch-chains. There would also be heavier tracks shaped like a trefoil, and they must have been made by a larger beast. These tracks ran right into the thicket, in among tree-trunks that had fallen to the wind.

'An elk has been here,' said Savushkin, as if talking about a close friend, when he saw that Anna Vasilevna was interested in the tracks.

'But don't be afraid,' he added in response to the glance the schoolmistress threw towards the depths of the forest, 'the deer is gentle.'

'Have you seen one?' asked Anna Vasilevna excitedly.

'No,' – Savushkin sighed. 'I haven't actually seen one, not alive. But I've seen his pellets.'

'Pellets?'

'Droppings,' Savushkin explained shyly.

Slipping under an archway of bent branches, the path again ran down to the stream. In some places the stream was covered with a thick white blanket of snow, while in others it was imprisoned in an armour of clear ice, and sometimes living water would gleam through the ice, looking like a dark, malevolent eye.

'Why has it not all frozen up?' asked Anna Vasilevna.

'There's a warm spring which rises up in it. Look! See that little jet?'

Bending over an unfrozen patch in the middle of the ice, Anna Vasilevna could see a thin little thread rising up from the bottom; by the time it reached the surface it had broken into tiny bubbles. This minute stem with the little bubbles on it looked like a spray of lily of the valley.

'There are loads of springs like that here,' said Savushkin enthusiastically. 'The stream is alive even under the snow.'

He brushed away the snow, and they saw the coal-black but transparent water.

Anna Vasilevna noticed that, when the snow fell into the water, it did not melt away, but immediately turned into slush, a greenish jelly suspended in the water as if it were algae. She was so pleased with this that she began to kick snow into the water with the toe of her boot, and was enraptured when a particularly intricate figure emerged from a large lump of snow. She was so enthralled that she did not at once notice that Savushkin had gone on, and was waiting for her, sitting high up in the fork of a bough overhanging the stream. Anna Vasilevna caught him up. Here the action of the warm springs came to an end, and the stream was covered with a thin film of ice. Light shadows darted rapidly over the marble surface.

'Look, the ice is so thin that we can even see the current!'

'No, Anna Vasilevna, I'm swaying this branch, and that's its shadow moving.'

Anna Vasilevna bit her tongue. Clearly here in the forest she had better keep quiet.

Savushkin strode on again in front of the schoolmistress, bending down slightly and looking around him.

And the forest led them on still farther along its intricate, tangled paths. It seemed as if there was no end to the trees, the snowdrifts and the silence of the sun-dappled twilight.

Suddenly, in the distance, a smoky-blue chink appeared. The trees began to thin out, there was more space and it was fresher. Soon there was no longer a chink, but a broad shaft of sunlight appeared before them, and in it something glistened and sparkled, swarming with frosty stars.

The path went round a hazel bush, and straightaway the forest fell away on either side. In the middle of the glade, clothed in glittering raiment, huge and majestic as a cathedral, stood an oak. It seemed as if the trees had respectfully stood aside to give their older brother room to display himself in all his strength. The lower branches spread out over the glade like a canopy.

Snow was packed into the deep corrugations of the bark, and the trunk, three times the normal girth, seemed to be embroidered with silver thread. Few of the leaves that had withered in the autumn had fallen, and the oak was covered right up to the top with leaves encased in snow.

'There it is, the winter oak!'

Yuri Nagibin

By answering the following questions, consider how the atmosphere the writer creates in this extract helps to convey the calm and magic of the countryside.

Exercise 1: 'The Winter Oak'

1 Give the meaning of these words as used in the passage:

submissively   trefoil   malevolent   enraptured   enthralled
corrugations

2 Explain as fully as you can what you learn about Anna Vasilevna and her reaction to what she sees and hears in the forest. You should refer closely to the passage in your answer.

3 Explain as fully as you can how Savushkin's behaviour in the forest helps you to understand him. Refer closely to the passage.

4 What do you think Anna Vasilevna learns from her experience in the forest?

5 Explain how the writer conveys the 'enchanted' nature of the forest by referring closely to some of the similes he uses in his description.

At the end of H.G. Wells's classic science-fiction story *The Time Machine*, the Time Traveller takes his machine millions of years into the future until he stops at a point when it seems as if the end of the world is soon to take place. Read this description from the book and then answer the questions that follow on page 6.

Extract 2: *The Time Machine*

Far away up the desolate slope I heard a harsh scream, and saw a thing like a huge white butterfly go slanting and fluttering up into the sky and, circling, disappear over some low hillocks beyond. The sound of its voice was so dismal that I shivered and seated myself more firmly upon the machine. Looking round me again, I saw that, quite near, what I had taken to be a reddish mass of rock was moving slowly towards me. Then I saw the thing was really a monstrous crab-like creature. Can you imagine a crab as large as yonder table, with its many legs moving slowly and uncertainly, its big claws swaying, its long antennae, like carters' whips, waving and feeling, and its stalked eyes gleaming at you on either side of its metallic front? Its back was corrugated and ornamented with ungainly bosses, and a greenish incrustation blotched it here and there. I could see the many palps of its complicated mouth flickering and feeling as it moved.

As I stared at this sinister apparition crawling towards me, I felt a tickling on my cheek as though a fly had lighted there. I tried to brush it away with my hand, but in a moment it returned, and almost immediately came another by my ear. I struck at this and caught something threadlike. It was drawn swiftly out of my hand. With a frightful qualm, I turned, and I saw that I had grasped the antenna of another monster crab that stood just behind me. Its evil eyes were wriggling on their stalks, its mouth was all alive with appetite, and its vast ungainly claws, smeared with an algal slime, were descending upon me. In a moment my hand was on the lever, and I had placed a month between myself and these monsters. But I was still on the same beach, and I saw them distinctly now as soon as I stopped. Dozens of them seemed to be crawling here and there, in the sombre light, among the foliated sheets of intense green.

I cannot convey the sense of abominable desolation that hung over the world. The red eastern sky, the northward blackness, the salt Dead Sea, the stony beach crawling with these foul, slow-stirring monsters, the uniform poisonous-looking green of the lichenous plants, the thin air that hurts one's lungs; all contributed to an appalling effect. I moved on a hundred years, and there was the same red sun – a little larger, a little duller – the same dying sea, the same chill air, and the same crowd of earthy crustacea creeping in and out among the green weed and the red rocks. And in the westward sky I saw a curved pale line like a vast new moon.

So I travelled, stopping ever and again, in great strides of a thousand years or more, drawn on by the mystery of the earth's fate, watching with a strange fascination the sun grow larger and duller in the westward sky, and the life of the old earth ebb away. At last, more than thirty million years hence, the huge red-hot dome of the sun had come to obscure nearly a tenth part of the darkling heavens. Then I stopped once more, for the crawling multitude of crabs had disappeared, and the red beach, save for its livid green liverworts and lichens, seemed lifeless. And now it was flecked with white. A bitter cold assailed me. Rare white flakes ever and again came eddying down. To the north-eastward, the glare of snow lay under the starlight of the sable sky, and I could see an undulating crest of hillocks pinkish white. There were fringes of ice along the sea margin, with drifting masses further out; but the main expanse of that salt ocean, all bloody under the eternal sunset, was still unfrozen.

I looked about me to see if any traces of animal life remained. A certain indefinable apprehension still kept me in the saddle of the machine. But I saw nothing moving, in earth or sky or sea. The green slime on the rocks alone testified that life was not extinct. A shallow sand-bank had appeared in the sea and the water had receded from the beach. I fancied I saw some black object flopping about upon this bank, but it became motionless *as I looked at it, and I judged that my eye had been deceived, and that the black object was merely a rock. The stars in the sky were intensely bright and seemed to me to twinkle very little.*

H.G. Wells

Exercise 2: The Time Machine

1 Explain the meaning of the following words as they are used in the extract:

   corrugated bosses incrustation palps sombre darkling sable apprehension

2 Describe, using your own words, the appearance of the monstrous crab mentioned in the first paragraph.

3 Which two words in the second paragraph describe the Time Traveller's fearful reaction to realising that he was being attacked by the second crab's antenna?

4 How did the Time Traveller escape from the crabs?

5 How many years into the future had the Time Traveller travelled by the end of his journey?

6 What is the only form of life that he found on earth at the end of his journey?

7 In the first three paragraphs, the narrator describes the 'abominable desolation' of the world of the distant future. Explain what you think is meant by this phrase. Then by looking closely at the words the writer uses to describe the landscape and the creatures that are part of it, explain how he creates this atmosphere.

8 In the final paragraphs, when the Traveller is at the end of his journey into the future, the atmosphere described by the writer has changed somewhat. By referring closely to the words and phrases he uses, explain this atmosphere and how it is suggested to the reader.

Bringing the past alive

One of the main tasks for writers of autobiography is to recreate the sights, sounds and smells of an earlier period of time to enable their readers to share in the experiences that they are describing. In the following passage, the Gibraltarian author Mary Chiappe recounts her memories of childhood visits to the fair held in La Linea – the Spanish town on the border of Gibraltar.

Read the passage carefully and then answer the questions that follow on page 9.

Extract 3: The fair at La Linea

My memories of the fairs I attended as a child are like the curate's egg – good in parts. Those were the days when new clothes made an appearance only on special occasions so I think I must have been excited by the prospect of a new dress; and I do remember a pair of white shoes that, try as I might, I never managed to keep clean among the press of people that thronged the dusty fairground. How often did we cross the frontier to La Linea during those nine days in July? On one of the days I know I would be decked out in the so-called gypsy dress – blood-red spots on a white background, the hem thick with ruffles that flared out as I walked. My face would be made up, my hair pulled back uncomfortably into a bun at the back of my neck and I was conscious that this was finery. I think I strutted a little as I walked and hoped people would notice how splendid I looked.

Way back in the late forties those fairs were tawdry affairs in a devastated Spain that struggled to emerge economically from the Civil War. In the circus everything looked moth-eaten, from the sad lions to the sequined costumes that didn't quite glitter. I feared for the trapeze artists; I couldn't find the clowns funny, try as I might; and the only thing I liked, possibly because my father liked them so much, were the little trained dogs that seemed happy as they performed small tricks to our applause. And we had waited so long for the show to start! None of the shows started on time. They couldn't afford to. Not till virtually all the seats had been sold did the performances finally begin. And all the time you were waiting, loud music blared out and battered your ears as if it was trying to convince you of an illusory *joie de vivre*. If nothing else, it anaesthetised your senses.

We seemed to call all the rides available 'los cacharros' – the whatsits. There were the tiny wooden 'cunitas', the cradles for toddlers, that swung to and fro sedately. There was the 'Ta-ta-chin', a miniature Ferris wheel with half a dozen child-containers. The most exciting thing about it was the name, which originated in the clashing cymbal and double drumbeat that was used, literally, to drum up trade. 'Chin!' went the cymbal. 'Ta-ta!' went the drum. There was also the large merry-go-round and its wonderful painted horses with their flaring nostrils and open red mouths, Oh, the disappointment when you were deemed too young to ride them and to hold on to the gleaming metal bar that anchored them to the carousel ceiling above you and allowed them to rise and fall as you were carried endlessly round, with the sights of the fair laid out before your eyes.

And the humble stalls that lined the streets sold small pieces of Spanish nougat, for who could afford a whole slab in those days? Others sold slivers of coconut as they still do today; and there was candyfloss that was fascinating to watch as the stallholder spun the sugary thread into a fluffy mass of bright pink. Pink, too, were the tiny sugary figures of animals on toothpicks, 'pirulines', that were impaled on a fleshy, prickly-pear leaf carried by itinerant sellers. Those leaves were also used to carry round a type of jasmine that drew moisture from the leaf and remained reasonably fresh for some young man to buy for his girlfriend.

My favourite stall was the one where they fried crisps on the spot and served them in 'cucuruchos' – brown paper cones – that they would twirl into shape with expert fingers and which, thanks to their shape, only contained a limited number of those curling, crackling potato delights. Yes, you've guessed it: I never felt I'd had enough of them. When I think of all the thin slices of potato kept below the stall in a bucket of water, and the number of times the oil was used and reused throughout the nine days, I can imagine that eating the crisps grew more hazardous with every passing day. And what of the ghastly lemonade? No flavour, just killer bubbles that attacked your throat and brought tears to your eyes?

The street lighting was feeble, but I had no complaints about it, and I loved the smell of grilled octopus and, as you finally left the fairground at two in the morning after coffee and 'churros' – cholesterol-laden fried batter – you might hear, from some bar, a voice that rose in the warm night air singing of love and betrayal. And, because that gypsy dress had become very, very heavy and you were only seven years old, you would end up being carried in your father's arms, your head drooping over his shoulder as you clutched a paper trumpet that you had bought from the easel-like stall covered in paper hats, little walking sticks and paper trumpets.

Innocent times. Perhaps I actually did like the fair after all.

Mary Chiappe

Exercise 3: The fair at La Linea

1 Explain the meaning of the following words and phrases as used in the passage:

strutted   tawdry   *joie de vivre*   anaesthetised your senses   sedately
slivers   itinerant

2 Explain carefully, using your own words, what the writer says in the first paragraph about the clothes that she had to wear.

3 Why didn't any of the shows start on time?

4 Explain, using your own words, what is meant by 'double drumbeat that was used, literally, to drum up trade'.

5 Why did eating the potato crisps become 'more hazardous with every passing day'?

6 What have you learnt about the food and drink that was on sale at the fair?

7 The writer says that her memories of the fair were 'good in parts'. Explain fully what she liked and disliked about it.

8 In the final paragraph, the writer switches from using the first-person pronoun 'I' to using the second-person pronoun 'you'. What effect does she achieve by this?

9 Select words and phrases from the passage which the writer uses to appeal to the reader's senses. Explain the effects of the words and phrases you have chosen.

10 At the end of the passage the writer refers to her memories as 'innocent times'. How is this sense of innocence conveyed by her writing?

Travel writing

Travel writers, in particular, want to create the atmosphere of the places they visit in the minds of their readers. Read the following extract in which Bill Bryson describes his impressions of the island of Capri and notice how he creates the atmosphere of the place, not just through describing what he sees but by appealing to the reader's other senses, especially that of smell.

Neither Here Nor There

A few of the lanes were enclosed, like catacombs, with the upper storeys of the houses completely covering the passageways. I followed one of these lanes now as it wandered upward through the town and finally opened again to the sky in a neighbourhood where the villas began to grow larger and enjoy more spacious grounds. The path meandered and climbed, so much so that I grew breathless again and propelled myself onwards by pushing my hands against my knees, but the scenery and setting were so fabulous that I was dragged on, as if by magnets. Near the top of the hillside the path levelled out and ran through a grove of pine trees, heavy with the smell of rising sap. On one side of the path were grand villas – I couldn't imagine by what method they got the furniture there when people moved in or out – and on the other was a giddying view of the island: white villas strewn across the hillsides, half buried in hibiscus and bougainvillaea and a hundred other types of shrub.

It was nearly dusk. A couple of hundred yards further on the path rounded a bend through the trees and ended suddenly, breathtakingly, in a viewing platform hanging out over a precipice of rock – a little patio in the sky. It was a look-out built for the public, but I had the feeling that no one had been there for years, certainly no tourist. It was the sheerest stroke of luck that I had stumbled on it. I have never seen anything half as beautiful: on one side the town of Capri spilling down the hillside, on the other the twinkling lights of the cove at Anacapri and the houses gathered around it, and in front of me a sheer drop of – what? – 200 feet, 300 feet, to a sea of the lushest aquamarine washing against outcrops of jagged rock. The sea was so far below that the sound of breaking waves reached me as the faintest of whispers. A sliver of moon, brilliantly white, hung in a pale blue evening sky, a warm breeze teased my hair and everywhere there was the scent of lemon, honeysuckle and pine. Ahead of me there was nothing but open sea, calm and seductive, for 150 miles to Sicily. I would do anything to own that view, anything.

Bill Bryson

Writing

> Activity
>
> Using the passage on page 10 as an example, write your own description of a place you know well. By concentrating on the sights, sounds and smells of the place, try to bring its atmosphere alive.

Reading for pleasure

Writers of stories of the supernatural and ghost stories depend very much on creating a suitably spooky atmosphere to provide a setting for the mysterious events that they recount. The following paragraphs are taken from the start of the classic supernatural tale 'The Fall of the House of Usher', by the nineteenth-century American author Edgar Allan Poe. As you read the description, think about how the writer not only creates the sinister atmosphere of the house itself and the surrounds, but also the apprehensive state of mind of the narrator. The words printed in italics are explained for you in the box to the right of the text on page 12.

'The Fall of the House of Usher'

During the whole of a dull, dark, and soundless day in the autumn of the year, when the clouds hung oppressively low in the heavens, I had been passing alone, on horseback, through a singularly dreary tract of country; and at length found myself, as the shades of the evening drew on, within view of the melancholy House of Usher. I know not how it was – but, with the first glimpse of the building, a sense of insufferable gloom pervaded my spirit. I say insufferable; for the feeling was unrelieved by any of that half-pleasurable, because poetic, sentiment, with which the mind usually receives even the sternest natural images of the desolate or terrible. I looked upon the scene before me – upon the mere house, and the simple landscape features of the domain – upon the bleak walls – upon the vacant eye-like windows – upon a few rank *sedges* – and upon a few white trunks of decayed trees – with an utter depression of soul ... There was an iciness, a sinking, a sickening of the heart – an unredeemed

This illustration created in 1938 depicts the destruction of the House of Usher later in the story

dreariness of thought which no goading of the imagination could torture into aught of the sublime. What was it – I paused to think – what was it that so unnerved me in the contemplation of the House of Usher? It was a mystery all insoluble; nor could I grapple with the shadowy fancies that crowded upon me as I pondered. I was forced to fall back upon the unsatisfactory conclusion, that while, beyond doubt, there are combinations of very simple natural objects which have the power of thus affecting us, still the analysis of this power lies among considerations beyond our depth. It was possible, I reflected, that a mere different arrangement of the particulars of the scene, of the details of the picture, would be sufficient to modify, or perhaps to annihilate its capacity for sorrowful impression; and, acting upon this idea, I reined my horse to the precipitous brink of a black and lurid *tarn* that lay in unruffled lustre by the dwelling, and gazed down – but with a shudder even more thrilling than before – upon the remodelled and inverted images of the grey sedge, and the ghastly tree-stems, and the vacant and eye-like windows.

Shaking off from my spirit what must have been a dream, I scanned more narrowly the real aspect of the building. Its principal feature seemed to be that of an excessive antiquity. The discoloration of ages had been great. Minute fungi overspread the whole exterior, hanging in a fine tangled web-work from the eaves. Yet all this was apart from any extraordinary dilapidation. No portion of the masonry had fallen; and there appeared to be a wild inconsistency between its

sedges	rush-like plants that grow near water and float on the surface
tarn	small lake
specious	deceptive in appearance

still perfect adaptation of parts, and the crumbling condition of the individual stones. In this there was much that reminded me of the *specious* totality of old wood-work which has rotted for long years in some neglected vault, with no disturbance from the breath of the external air. Beyond this indication of extensive decay, however, the fabric gave little token of instability. Perhaps the eye of a scrutinising observer might have discovered a barely perceptible fissure, which, extending from the roof of the building in front, made its way down the wall in a zigzag direction, until it became lost in the sullen waters of the tarn.

The room in which I found myself was very large and lofty. The windows were long, narrow, and pointed, and at so vast a distance from the black oaken floor as to be altogether inaccessible from within. Feeble gleams of encrimsoned light made their way through the trellised panes, and served to render sufficiently distinct the more prominent objects around. The eye, however, struggled in vain to reach the remoter angles of the chamber, or the recesses of the vaulted and fretted ceiling. Dark draperies hung upon the walls. The general furniture was profuse, comfortless, antique, and tattered. Many books and musical instruments lay scattered about, but failed to give any vitality to the scene. I felt that I breathed an atmosphere of sorrow. An air of stern, deep, and irredeemable gloom hung over and pervaded all.

Edgar Allan Poe

Speaking and listening

Activity

Think of a place that you like to go to when you feel the need to be alone – it could be a quiet spot in the countryside, an old building or simply a room in your house/ apartment or a part of your school. Give a talk about the place to your class, concentrating on creating its special atmosphere which makes it so attractive to you.

Key skills

Punctuation

Semi-colons and colons

These are both important punctuation devices, and the ability to use them confidently and correctly is a mark of a competent writer. Although their names are similar, their functions are distinctly different. The **semi-colon** is used for two main purposes:

1 To separate two main clauses when a conjunction such as *and* or *but* is omitted:

When I woke up, I remembered that I had a particularly demanding Maths test this morning; I really did not want to get out of bed.

2 To separate groups of words in a list (clauses or sentences) inside which commas may already exist:

I started to pack my bag ready for school. I packed my trusty calculator, the screen cracked by an earlier accident; two spare pencils, in case the one I was using broke its point; my geometry instruments, which my grandfather had given me; a book entitled *Mathematics Made Simple*, written by I. Countem; and my good-luck charm in case all else failed!

Note: In the first example above, it would be incorrect to use a comma instead of the semi-colon as a comma is not strong enough to separate two main clauses. It would not be wrong to use a conjunction such as *and* instead of the semi-colon but doing so would reduce the emphatic impact of the second half of the sentence.

A **colon** has three specific uses, and is a less flexible punctuation device than the semi-colon. It is used:

1 To separate two clauses where the second explains more fully the meaning of the first:

I really did not want to get out of bed that morning: I had a very demanding Maths test that day and had done very little revision.

2 To introduce a number of items in a list:

The following items were to be found in my school bag: my trusty calculator, two spare pencils, my geometry instruments, a book entitled *Mathematics Made Simple* and my good-luck charm.

3 To introduce a speech or quotation:

Hamlet: To be, or not to be, that is the question.

Exercise: Semi-colons and colons

Copy the following sentences and add semi-colons and colons where necessary:

1 There are two main reasons for your disappointing performance this term you have not completed all your homework assignments and you have spent too much time dreaming during lessons.

2 Rita did not want to go to bed when her mother told her to she really wanted to watch the late-night film on television.

3 In order to visit his grandparents, Hari had to walk to the nearest bus stop which was 800 metres from his home wait half an hour for the next bus as he had just missed one stand up on the journey as the bus was crowded change to another equally crowded bus and then walk for fifteen minutes to their house.

4 Am I right in thinking that these were your actual words I really can't be bothered to do my science homework tonight?

5 In order to make pancakes you will need the following items eggs, flour, water and milk.

6 Remember it is important not to panic when reading exam questions.

7 It was six o'clock in the morning the sun was just beginning to rise.

8 When cooking your pancakes you should sift the flour into a bowl making sure that you don't spill any break two eggs into a cup to check they are fresh add the eggs to the flour which is in the bowl whisk them together gradually adding milk and water as you do so.

9 It was too late the phone stopped ringing just as he picked up the receiver.

10 Men are from Mars women are from Venus.

Errors to avoid

In Chapter 8 we will be looking at how the English language developed. One of the main points about English is that because it has absorbed many different influences over the centuries, it has become a very flexible language which enables writers to express a wide range of thoughts and feelings. However, a problem associated with this flexibility is that it is difficult to formulate a precise set of rules on how to use the English language correctly. Here, and later in this book, we will look at some of the areas of English expression that cause most confusion and give tips on how to avoid them.

Errors of agreement

It is important that subjects and their verbs should agree in number: both should be singular or both plural. Sometimes, especially in a complex sentence, it is very easy to get this wrong. For example, in the following sentence, the writer has forgotten that the subject of the sentence (*library*) is singular because of the number of plural nouns that come between it and the verb (*were*):

> The library, full of books, computers, printers, DVD collections, and magazines, were very much in need of tidying up.

Wrongly used prepositions

Prepositions are words that are placed usually before nouns or pronouns to indicate some relation, for example *in, on, to, at*. Using these precisely is essential in order to express yourself accurately. For example, 'He sat by the cat' has a different meaning from 'He sat on the cat'.

Misusing nouns ending in –s

Some nouns – the items of clothing known as *jeans* and *pants*, for example – are grammatically plural forms and do not have singular forms. It is, therefore, *incorrect* to write:

> He tore his pant as he climbed over the wall.

> She washed her jean after she fell in the mud.

Tautology

Tautology is saying exactly the same thing more than once, especially within the same sentence. For example:

> At the end of the party the children returned back home.

> The true facts of the incident are as follows.

In these sentences the words *back* and *true* are unnecessary: *return* means 'go back' and *facts* are, by definition, true.

Confusing similar words

Many writers of English blur the meaning of what they want to say by confusing words that either sound similar or have a similar but not exactly equivalent meaning. Here are some of these words:

- avoid/prevent
- stay/live
- bring/take
- uninterested/disinterested
- bored/boring
- there/their/they're
- your/you're
- horde/hoard
- principal/principle
- affect/effect.

Exercise: Choosing the right word

Write sentences containing each of the words listed above to make their meaning clear. Remember: if you are in doubt about their meanings, check them in a dictionary before writing your sentences.

Reading

A diary is an individual's personal account of his/her daily experiences. Very often, diaries contain not just details of what happened on particular days, but also include observations and thoughts inspired by the events recorded.

It is very likely that many of you have tried to keep a diary at some time or other and equally likely that many of you gave up, either because keeping it going became too much of a chore or because you felt that what you were recording was of little interest. However, others among you may still be keeping a regular account of your activities in diary form and discovering the value of being able to express your private thoughts and feelings, knowing that they are not intended to be shared with anyone else.

Although some people, such as politicians, keep diaries in order to explain and justify their contributions to important events and with the intention that their diaries will one day be published, not all diaries are written for this purpose. Most people keep diaries for precisely the opposite reason – they want what they write to be kept secret and to be seen by their eyes only because they use their diaries as an opportunity to express their most intimate thoughts and feelings about their experiences and the people they meet. The extracts that follow on pages 18–21 are taken from two such diaries.

The first extract is by the seventeenth-century writer Samuel Pepys (pronounced *peeps*). Pepys was a quite important civil servant who lived in London at the time of King Charles II; he worked in the Admiralty Office and kept a diary in which he recorded both public events and also details of his personal life and experiences. He wrote his diary in a form of code and had no intention that it would ever be published. However, after his death, his diaries were found and translated. They give us not just a unique insight into some of the great historical events of the time, but also an intimate understanding of the thoughts and attitudes of an individual human who was alive 350 years ago. This extract describes the Great Fire of London in 1666.

Read the extract carefully and the answer the questions that follow on page 19.

Extract 1: Samuel Pepys's diary

(Lord's day). Some of our mayds sitting up late last night to get things ready against [in preparation for] our feast to-day, Jane called us up about three in the morning, to tell us of a great fire they saw in the City. So I rose and slipped on my nightgowne, and went to her window, and thought it to be on the backside of Marke-lane at the farthest; but, being unused to such fires as followed, I thought it far enough off; and so went to bed again and to sleep.

About seven rose again to dress myself, and there looked out at the window, and saw the fire not so much as it was and further off ... By and by Jane comes and tells me that she hears that above 300 houses have been burned down to-night by the fire we saw, and that it is now burning down all Fish-street, by London Bridge. So I made myself ready presently, and walked to the Tower [of London], and there got up upon one of the high places, Sir J. Robinson's little son going up with me; and there I did see the houses at that end of the bridge all on fire, and an infinite great fire on this and the other side the end of the bridge; which, among other people, did trouble me for poor little Michell and our Sarah on the bridge. So down, with my heart full of trouble, to the Lieutenant of the Tower, who tells me that it begun this morning in the King's baker's house in Pudding-lane, and that it hath burned St Magnus's Church and most part of Fish-street already.

So I down to the water-side, and there got a boat and through bridge, and there saw a lamentable fire. Poor Michell's house, as far as the Old Swan, already burned that way, and the fire running further, that in a very little time it got as far as the Steele-yard, while I was there. Everybody endeavouring to remove their goods, and flinging into the river or bringing them into lighters [flat-bottomed boats] that layoff; poor people staying in their houses as long as till the very fire touched them, and then running into boats, or clambering from one pair of stairs by the water-side to another. And among other things, the poor pigeons,

I perceive, were loth to leave their houses, but hovered about the windows and balconys till they were, some of them burned, their wings, and fell down. Having staid, and in an hour's time seen the fire rage every way, and nobody, to my sight, endeavouring to quench it, but to remove their goods, and leave all to the fire, and having seen it get as far as the Steele-yard, and the wind mighty high and driving it into the City; and every thing, after so long a drought, proving combustible, even the very stones of churches, and among other things the poor steeple by which pretty Mrs ————— lives, and whereof my old school-fellow Elborough is parson, taken fire in the very top, an there burned till it fell down: I to White Hall (with a gentleman with me who desired to go off from the Tower, to see the fire, in my boat); to White Hall, and there up to the Kings closett in the Chappell, where people come about me, and did give them an account dismayed them all, and word was carried in to the King. So I was called for, and did tell the King and Duke of Yorke what I saw, and that unless his Majesty did command houses to be pulled down nothing could stop the fire.

They seemed much troubled, and the King commanded me to go to my Lord Mayor from him, and command him to spare no houses, but to pull down before the fire every way. The Duke of York bid me tell him that if he would have any more soldiers he shall … Here meeting, with Captain Cocke, I in his coach, which he lent me, and Creed with me to [St] Paul's [Cathedral], and there walked along Watlingstreet, as well as I could, every creature coming away loaden with goods to save, and here and there sicke people carried away in beds. Extraordinary good goods carried in carts and on backs. At last met my Lord Mayor in Canningstreet, like a man spent, with a handkercher about his neck. To the King's message he cried, like a fainting woman, 'Lord! what can I do? I am spent: people will not obey me. I have been pulling down houses; but the fire overtakes us faster than we can do it.' That he needed no more soldiers; and that, for himself, he must go and refresh himself, having been up all night. So he left me, and I him, and walked home, seeing people all almost distracted, and no manner of means used to quench the fire. The houses, too, so very thick thereabouts, and full of matter for burning, as pitch and tar, in Thames-street; and warehouses of oil, and wines, and brandy, and other things.

Samuel Pepys

Exercise 1: Samuel Pepys's diary

1 Where did Samuel Pepys think that the fire had begun and who told him it had started?
2 Explain what Pepys means by referring to the fire as 'lamentable'.
3 What were most people doing instead of trying to put out the fire?
4 What two things does Pepys say were making the fire worse?
5 What did Pepys tell the King that he should do in order to try to stop the fire?
6 Using your own words, describe the state of mind of the Lord Mayor.
7 At the end of the extract what other reasons does Pepys give for why the fire was spreading so fiercely?

The following extracts are from the diary kept by a young Dutch Jewish girl, Anne Frank, who lived in hiding from the Nazis with her family in Amsterdam during the Second World War. Anne's diary (which she called 'Kitty') includes details of Anne's life and reveals the thoughts and feelings of an extraordinary schoolgirl trying to live an ordinary life under a tyranny. Again, this diary was never intended for publication.

Read the extracts carefully and then answer the questions that follow on page 21.

Extract 2: Anne Frank's diary

Monday, 26 July 1943

Dearest Kitty,

Yesterday was a very tumultuous day, and we're still all wound up. Actually, you may wonder if there's ever a day that passes without some kind of excitement.

The first warning siren went off in the morning while we were at breakfast, but we paid no attention, because it only meant that the planes were crossing the coast. I had a terrible headache, so I lay down for an hour after breakfast and then went to the office at about two. At two-thirty Margot had finished her office work and was just gathering her things together when the sirens began wailing again. So she and I trooped back upstairs. None too soon, it seems, for less than five minutes later the guns were booming so loudly that we went and stood in the passage. The house shook and the bombs kept falling. I was clutching my 'escape bag', more because I wanted to have something to hold on to than because I wanted to run away. I know we can't leave here, but if we had to, being seen on the streets would be just as dangerous as getting caught in an air raid. After half an hour the drone of engines faded and the house began to hum with activity again. Peter emerged from his lookout post in the front attic, Dussel remained in the front office, Mrs van D. felt safest in the private office, Mr van Daan had been watching from the loft, and those of us on the landing spread out to watch the columns of smoke rising from the harbour. Before long the smell of fire was everywhere, and outside it looked as if the city were enveloped in a thick fog.

A big fire like that is not a pleasant sight, but fortunately for us it was all over, and we went back to our various jobs. Just as we were starting dinner: another air-raid alarm. The food was good, but I lost my appetite the moment I heard the siren. Nothing happened, however, and forty-five minutes later the all-clear was sounded. After the washing-up: another air-raid warning, gunfire and swarms of planes. 'Oh gosh, twice in one day,' we thought, 'that's twice too many.' Little good that did us, because once again the bombs rained down, this time on the other side of the city. According to British reports, Schiphol Airport was bombed. The planes dived and climbed, the air was abuzz with the drone of engines. It was very scary, and the whole time I kept thinking, 'Here it comes, this is it.'

I can assure you that when I went to bed at nine, my legs were still shaking. At the stroke of midnight I woke up again: more planes! Dussel was undressing, but I took no notice and leapt up, wide awake, at the sound of the first shot. I stayed in Father's bed until one, in my own bed until one-thirty, and was back in Father's bed at two. But the planes kept on coming.

It's utterly impossible for me to build my life on a foundation of chaos, suffering and death. I see the world being slowly transformed into a wilderness, I hear the approaching thunder that, one day, will destroy us too, I feel the suffering of millions. And yet, when I look up at the sky, I somehow feel that everything will change for the better, that this cruelty too will end, that peace and tranquillity will return once more. In the meantime, I must hold on to my ideals. Perhaps the day will come when I'll be able to realise them!

I feel wicked sleeping in a warm bed, while somewhere out there my dearest friends are dropping from exhaustion or being knocked to the ground. I get frightened myself when I think of close friends who are now at the mercy of the cruellest monsters ever to stalk the earth. And all because they're Jews.

Anne Frank

Exercise 2: *Anne Frank's diary*

1 Why does Anne Frank say the sirens were sounding?
2 Explain in your own words Anne's comment about her 'escape bag'.
3 What details from the first extract from Anne's diary tell you that the Frank family and their friends were having to keep a close watch out for fear of being discovered?
4 What details tell you that Anne was scared by the events she describes in the first extract?
5 By referring to all the extracts from Anne Frank's diary explain as fully as you can what you have learnt about her character and the situation she was in.

Exercise 3: Comparing diary extracts

Write a detailed comparison of the diary extracts by Samuel Pepys and Anne Frank. In particular, you should think about the events they describe, the other people they refer to and the personal comments and reflections they contain.

Writing to analyse and comment

The extracts from diaries that you have just read contain not only details of what happened on a particular day, but also the writers' thoughts about their experiences. Keeping a diary or journal not intended to be read by anyone else (let alone published) allows writers to explore their thoughts and feelings about issues in a unique way.

If you keep a diary yourself, it is a good idea to use it as an opportunity to write at some length and explore your own thoughts about a particular topic. Being able to write analytically about what you have experienced is a key skill. For example, you may read a book or watch a film that you find enjoyable or emotionally engaging, but explaining what it was that caused you to be affected in such a way (so that you can share the experience with your friends, perhaps) is something that is not easy to do. In order to be able to express clearly your thoughts or feelings about something, you need to be able to put them into words so that you can understand them yourself. Writing in a diary is one way to practise doing this without the concern that someone else will read and criticise what you have written. Don't worry about going on at length in order to understand fully your thoughts about an issue – once you become familiar with analysing your feelings, expressing them in a more focused way will become a lot easier. However, you are unlikely to reach this stage if you do not allow yourself to develop your thoughts at length by exploring them fully.

Now read this poem by the Jamaican poet A.L. Hendriks. It is followed by a student's essay about the poem.

'Road to Lacovia'

This is a long, forbidding road, a narrow,
hard aisle of asphalt under
a high gothic arch of bamboos.
Along it a woman drags a makeshift barrow
in slanting rain, and thunder:
a thin woman who wears no shoes.

This is St Elizabeth, a hard parish
to work; but when you are born
on land, you want to work that land.
Nightfall comes here swift and harsh and deep, but garish
flames of lightning show up torn
cheap clothing barely patched, and

a face patterned by living. Every sharp line
of this etching has the mark
of struggle. To the eye, unyielding
bleak earth has brought her close to famine;
yet through this wild descent of dark
this woman dares to walk, and sing.

A.L. Hendriks

Read through the following essay and consider how clearly it conveys the student's response to the poem.

I like this poem. It makes you think about the hard lives of people who live in country areas. It describes a woman pulling a 'makeshift barrow' along a long, narrow road. It is raining hard and the woman, who is thin, is not wearing shoes.

In the second verse, the poem tells us that the scene is in St Elizabeth, an area of Jamaica. Lacovia is a town in the parish of St Elizabeth. The poet describes it as 'a hard parish to work'. It isn't clear if this means that work is hard in the area or that it is hard to find work there, perhaps it has both meanings. It also says that if you are born on this land, then you want to work that land. The last three lines of this verse tell us that nightfall comes quickly here and there also seems to be a thunderstorm as it says that the lightning shows us the woman's face which has been 'patterned by living' and the cheap clothing that she is wearing.

In the last verse, the poet repeats that the woman's life is hard, and that she is 'close to famine', which means that she can't have much to eat. However, she is singing as she walks and this would seem to suggest that she is happy, though I'm not sure why.

The poem consists of three verses of six lines each and in each verse the words rhyme (line 1 with line 4, line 2 with line 5 and line 3 with line 6). Many of the words in the poem remind us of the harsh life the woman lives ('forbidding', 'hard', 'harsh', 'bleak', 'struggle', 'cheap', 'bleak', 'famine'). The poem also talks about the cruel weather and how the 'garish lightning' shows up the woman's cheap, patched clothes and the lines 'etched' on her face.

Overall, this essay shows that the student has a quite good understanding of the poem as a whole, but you probably noticed that some of the comments lack detailed development and that they tend to record points rather than explain them. Now look at the essay again with the teacher's comments added:

Good, but will you make it clear why you like it?

Good point, but it would help if you explored further the implications of the two meanings.

You need to ask yourself 'Why?' and then explain your answer as this last line contains the poem's main message. Try to explain fully the meaning of this last sentence, starting from 'To the eye, unyielding bleak earth ...'. What does it tell us about the woman's spirit?

Again, you have referred to the poet's choice of words without really developing any of your comments. It would help to explain how these words reinforce the picture of the woman's life.

I like this poem. It makes you think about the hard lives of people who live in country areas. It describes a woman pulling a 'makeshift barrow' along a long, narrow road. It is raining hard and the woman, who is thin, is not wearing shoes.

In the second verse, the poem tells us that the scene is in St Elizabeth, an area of Jamaica. Lacovia is a town in the parish of St Elizabeth. The poet describes it as 'a hard parish to work'. It isn't clear if this means that work is hard in the area or that it is hard to find work there, perhaps it has both meanings. It also says that if you are born on this land, then you want to work that land. The last three lines of this verse tell us that nightfall comes quickly here and there also seems to be a thunderstorm as it says that the lightning shows us the woman's face which has been 'patterned by living' and the cheap clothing that she is wearing.

In the last verse, the poet repeats that the woman's life is hard, and that she is 'close to famine', which means that she can't have much to eat. However, she is singing as she walks and this would seem to suggest that she is happy, though I'm not sure why.

The poem consists of three verses of six lines each and in each verse the words rhyme (line 1 with line 4, line 2 with line 5 and line 3 with line 6). Many of the words in the poem remind us of the harsh life the woman lives ('forbidding', 'hard', 'harsh', 'bleak', 'struggle', 'cheap', 'bleak', 'famine'). The poem also talks about the cruel weather and how the 'garish lightning' shows up the woman's cheap, patched clothes and the lines 'etched' on her face.

What does the description of the woman and her barrow suggest about the life she leads?

How does the poem describe the lightning? What is suggested by the word 'garish'? You could also comment more about what it reveals about her clothing. The rain is also described as 'slanting' in the first verse – it would be a good idea to refer to that in your comment as well.

Rather than describing the way the poem rhymes, try to comment on the effect. Does the rhyme emphasise certain key words in the poem?

What is 'etching'? Why is this choice of word particularly apt here?

25

Reading for pleasure

Sometimes, authors will use the form of a diary for fictional purposes. Here are some extracts from *The Diary of a Nobody* by the brothers George and Weedon Grossmith. It is the fictional diary of the mundane and uninteresting life of the rather self-important office clerk Charles Pooter, his family (wife, Carrie, and son, Lupin) and friends. Pooter's diary provides us with a comic picture of middle-class life in England in the late nineteenth century.

The Diary of a Nobody

APRIL 8. No events of any importance, except that Gowing strongly recommended a new patent stylographic pen, which cost me nine-and-sixpence, and which was simply nine-and-sixpence thrown in the mud. It has caused me constant annoyance and irritability of temper. The ink oozes out of the top, making a mess on my hands, and once at the office when I was knocking the palm of my hand on the desk to jerk the ink down, Mr Perkupp, who had just entered, called out: 'Stop that knocking! I suppose that is you, Mr Pitt?' That young monkey, Pitt, took a malicious glee in responding quite loudly: 'No, sir; I beg pardon, it is Mr Pooter with his pen; it has been going on all the morning.' To make matters worse, I saw Lupin laughing behind his desk. I thought it wiser to say nothing. I took the pen back to the shop and asked them if they would take it back, as it did not act. I did not expect the full price returned, but was willing to take half. The man said he could not do that – buying and selling were two different things. Lupin's conduct during the period he has been in Mr Perkupp's office has been most exemplary. My only fear is, it is too good to last.

Charles Pooter

Lupin Pooter

APRIL 9. Gowing called, bringing with him an invitation for Carrie and myself to a ball given by the East Acton Rifle Brigade, which he thought would be a swell affair, as the member for East Acton (Sir William Grime) had promised his patronage. We accepted of his kindness, and he stayed to supper, an occasion I thought suitable for trying a bottle of the sparkling Algéra that Mr James (of Sutton) had sent as a present. Gowing sipped the wine, observing that he had never tasted it before, and further remarked that his policy was to stick to more recognised brands. I told him it was a present from a dear friend, and one mustn't look a gift-horse in the mouth. Gowing facetiously replied: 'And he didn't like putting it in the mouth either.'

I thought the remarks were rude without being funny, but on tasting it myself, came to the conclusion there was some justification for them. The sparkling Algéra is very like cider, only more sour. I suggested that perhaps the thunder had turned it a bit acid. He merely replied: 'Oh! I don't think so.' We had a very pleasant game of cards, though I lost four shillings and Carrie lost one, and Gowing said he had lost about sixpence: how he could have lost, considering that Carrie and I were the only other players, remains a mystery.

APRIL 14, SUNDAY. Owing, I presume, to the unsettled weather, I awoke with a feeling that my skin was drawn over my face as tight as a drum. Walking round the garden with Mr and Mrs Treane, members of our congregation who had walked back with us, I was much annoyed to find a large newspaper full of bones on the gravel-path, evidently thrown over by those young Griffin boys next door; who, whenever we have friends, climb up the empty steps inside their conservatory, tap at the windows, making faces, whistling, and imitating birds.

APRIL 15. Burnt my tongue most awfully with the Worcester sauce, through that stupid girl Sarah shaking the bottle violently before putting it on the table.

George and Weedon Grossmith

Writing

Activity

Now it's your opportunity to write a diary or journal entry. Here are some suggestions:
- Write a diary account of two ordinary days of your school life. Try to take a humorous approach to this, in the manner of *The Diary of a Nobody*, so that you appear to give great importance to the most mundane events.
- Write imaginary diary entries for a character from a book, film or television programme that you have enjoyed. Again, you could take a humorous approach to this or treat the task more seriously to show your understanding of the character and his/her behaviour.

Speaking and listening

> Pair activity
>
> Working with a friend, give an account of an activity in which you both took part. Taking it in turns, one of you should recount the version of events that you would like to tell to an adult (for example, your parents or a teacher) then the other person should give the account of the same event that you recorded in your diary, which no one else is supposed to read!

Key skills

Punctuation

Commas

In *Student's Book 1* we looked at different occasions when commas should be used. Now we are going to look at one further use of the comma. This use is a particularly tricky one:

- A comma is used to separate from the rest of the sentence a group of words that act as an adjective and that begin with 'who', 'whom', 'which' or 'that' *but only when this group of words has a non-defining function.*

Here are some examples to help you understand what this means and how the 'rule' works. In the following sentence, the words in italics function together as an adjective describing the car:

The car, *which was old and rusty*, belonged to the school teacher.

Here the words *which was old and rusty* give us additional information about the car, but we do not need this information to understand the main point of the sentence (that the car belonged to the teacher).

Now look at this sentence:

The car *that was involved in the robbery* belonged to the teacher.

This time the words in italics define the car and are essential to the meaning of the sentence – without them we would not know which car is being talked about.

Dashes and hyphens

The **dash** has a variety of uses. Its main use is to indicate an interruption to the main structure of a sentence, for example by an afterthought or by words interjected into the sentence. A dash is placed before and after these words – unless the interruption comes at the end of a sentence, when a full stop, question mark or exclamation mark replaces the second dash. For example:

> She showed me her new dress – very nice it was too – that her parents had given her for her thirteenth birthday.

> She showed me her new dress that her parents had given her for her thirteenth birthday – and very nice it was too!

Another use of the dash is to indicate a sudden dramatic end to a sentence:

> 'I'll tell you who the culprit was,' said the Headteacher. 'It was – the School Librarian.'

Finally, a dash can be used to show when a word or sentence is incomplete:

> The police made sure the identity of Mr K– was kept secret.

> 'Help. Help, I'm –' he shouted, but he fell off the ladder before I could reach him!

A **hyphen** has two uses. It is a device for linking compound words together. For example the phrase 'fine-tooth comb' means a comb with fine teeth (very thin teeth that are close together); on the other hand 'a fine tooth-comb' (if such an item existed) would describe an unusual dental implement which would be used to comb teeth – as an alternative to a toothbrush, perhaps!

The hyphen is also used to divide a word into syllables when there is not room to fit the complete word into the space at the end of a line.

A dash can be distinguished from a hyphen as it is slightly longer.

Exercise: Punctuation

Copy and punctuate the following passage, using whatever punctuation is required.

> they had been walking for hours the weather was hot and humid and lees thoughts were very much focused on the cool shower that he would have when they finally reached the place where they were going to spend the night or at least he hoped that the camp site where they were staying would have some showers ahead of them was a steep hill which they would have to climb lee looked at his watch and saw that it was three oclock in the afternoon they all sighed as they approached the hill but suddenly they heard a sound in the distance it was an old toyota truck which was coming towards them as it drew alongside the driver slowed down and called from his window hey you kids do you want a lift im going as far as the campsite on the other side of the hill lee and his friends had climbed into the back of the truck before the driver had finished speaking

Reading

Myths and legends are traditional stories that are associated with different countries. Many myths contain some details that are historical facts that have been added to and romanticised over the centuries. Many places throughout the world have particular legendary stories associated with them. Although the origins of some of these stories are lost in the mists of time, other stories are more recent and, indeed, myths and legends are continuing to develop in the present day.

Four accounts of myths and legends from different countries and from different ages follow on pages 30–36. Some are well known, others less so. The first example comes from a tourist information guide to the island of Langkawi in Malaysia.

Read this extract carefully and then answer the questions that follow on page 31.

Extract 1: Legends of Langkawi

The legends associated with Langkawi are very old and known to have existed since ancient times. Many of these legends are vague in their origins and have lost their appeal over the years; but some have survived the test of time and are fresh in the minds of the people of Langkawi. Most of the places often frequented by people have a tale or legend of their own which make them more special with an added attraction.

The best-known legend of Langkawi is of Mahsuri, a pretty maiden who lived during the reign of Sultan Abdullah Mukarram Shah the Second, who ruled Kedah between 1762 and 1800. She died under tragic circumstances for a crime she did not commit. She died a victim of a conspiracy plotted against her out of jealousy by Mahura, her very own mother-in-law, for her magnetic personality. Mahura had bitterly objected to her husband's intention of taking Mahsuri as his second wife and eventually agreed that their son, Mat Deris, should seek the hand of Mahsuri in marriage. Since then, Mahura had grown bitterly jealous of Mahsuri, for whom she bore much hatred.

Mahsuri's tomb, Langkawi

In time, Mahsuri gave birth to a baby boy and he was named Mat Arus. This inflamed Mahura even more. Mahsuri was accused of committing adultery with Deramang, a young troubadour whom she befriended. The chieftain of Langkawi, Datuk Seri Kerma Jaya, Mahsuri's own father-in-law, was so taken in by Mahura's accusation that, without a proper investigation, he sentenced Mahsuri to death.

As proof of her innocence, some people say, white blood was seen gushing out of her wound during execution at Padang Hangus. Others maintain there was the sudden appearance of white mist that enveloped the spot where she was executed, which it was believed was a sign of mourning of her innocence.

Mahsuri is best remembered for her curse on Langkawi which was uttered before she died. She said, 'For this act of injustice Langkawi shall not prosper for seven generations to come.' The execution of Mahsuri was indeed a tragedy of dramatic proportions. And her curse? Myth, legend or fantasy? History tells us that within a few years of Mahsuri's death, Langkawi was devastated by the Siamese and Datuk Seri Kerma Jaya and his entire family were killed. Rice fields and granaries were completely set on fire.

To this day, grains that appear to be burnt rice grains are still to be found at Padang Matsirat, a small town in Langkawi. However, many believe the curse is now over with the numerous development projects undertaken on the island.

Exercise 1: Legends of Langkawi

1 Explain the meaning of 'conspiracy'.
2 Deramang is described as a young 'troubadour'. What exactly is a troubadour?
3 What were the legendary signs that Mahsuri was innocent?
4 According to the passage, what suggestions are there that there may be some truth in this legend?
5 Langkawi has now become a popular tourist destination. Do you think that the legend may in any way help the popularity of the resort? Give your reasons.

Many myths and legends tell stories of fights against monsters and dragons. Here is one of the myths of ancient Greece. Read this story carefully and then answer the questions that follow on page 33.

Extract 2: Theseus and the Minotaur

Prince Theseus was the son of King Aegeus of Athens, not too long before the Trojan War (so maybe around 1300BCE). At this time the Minoans, who lived on the island of Crete, had a very strong navy. The Minoan king, King Minos, used to send his navy to attack Greek cities, including Athens. Everyone was afraid of him and his soldiers.

King Aegeus had an agreement with King Minos that if Minos would leave Athens alone, Aegeus would send seven Athenian boys and seven Athenian girls to Crete every nine years, to be eaten by a monster that lived on Crete, the Minotaur. They had been doing this for a long time, but of course the boys and girls who had to go to be eaten and their mums and dads hated it!

One day it was once again time to send the children to Crete. Everyone was crying. Prince Theseus said that he was going to go with them and kill the Minotaur, to save these children and all the ones who might be sent in the future. His dad, King Aegeus, begged him not to go. Aegeus was afraid that the Minotaur would get Theseus too! But Theseus said he was going to go, and he got on the boat. The boat had a black sail, to show how sad everyone was. King Aegeus made Theseus promise to change to a white sail if he lived to come home, to announce that he had won, and Theseus promised.

When they got to Crete, King Minos and his daughter Princess Ariadne [arr-ee-AD-nee] came out of their palace to see Theseus and the other Athenian children. King Minos just said to throw them in to the Minotaur the next day, but Ariadne fell in love with Theseus (yes, just like that!) and she wanted to help him.

So late that night Ariadne gave Theseus a sword and a ball of string. She told him to tie the string to the door of the Labyrinth where the Minotaur lived (a big maze) and unroll it behind him as he went so he could find his way back out, and to use the sword to kill the Minotaur. Theseus thanked Ariadne very much and promised to marry her if he escaped without being eaten by the Minotaur.

Theseus and the Minotaur – Athenian black-figure vase, about 550BCE

The next morning all the Athenians went into the Labyrinth. The others were afraid, but Prince Theseus tied the string to the door and went to find the

Minotaur. Finally he did find the Minotaur and there was a big fight, but then Theseus killed the Minotaur with his sword and followed the string back to the door. The other Athenians were very happy to see him and to hear that he had killed the Minotaur!

Princess Ariadne opened the door and let them out, and they all ran away to their ship and sailed away: Theseus, Ariadne, and all the other Athenians.

But when Theseus and Ariadne got to the island of Delos, halfway home from Crete, they stopped to rest. Ariadne fell asleep, and Theseus left her there on the island and sailed away to Athens without her. Different Greek stories give different reasons why he did this: maybe he just didn't like her very much, or maybe he thought the Athenians wouldn't like her because she was Cretan. Or maybe he was afraid King Minos would be angry. Some stories say it was because Dionysos fell in love with her. But all the stories agree that he left her there on the island.

When Theseus got as far as Sounion, he was close enough for the ship to be seen from Athens. But he had forgotten to change the sail from black to white! His father, King Aegeus, was looking out for Theseus' ship. When he saw the black sail he thought Theseus was dead, and he was so sad that he jumped off the cliff and killed himself.

Exercise 2: Theseus and the Minotaur

1 At the time of the story, who were the kings of Athens and Crete?
2 Using your own words, explain the agreement that had been made between the Athenians and the Minoans.
3 What was the promise Theseus made to his father before he left for Crete?
4 What was the Minotaur and where did it live?
5 Explain fully how Theseus escaped from the Minotaur.
6 What impressions do you get of the character of Theseus from this account?
7 What evidence can you find in the way that this story is told that this version was originally written for young children?

Not to be outdone, the county of Cornwall in the United Kingdom has its own mysterious myths. Many of these are associated with the legendary King Arthur, but more recent myths are still arising from this region. On page 34 is an extract from a tourist guide to Cornwall which tells of a much more modern mythical monster than the Minotaur. Read this extract carefully and then answer the questions that follow on page 35.

Extract 3: The Beast of Bodmin

There is no doubt that Bodmin Moor is a creepy place. Should you happen to find yourself alone there as dusk is falling, try not to think about the layers of legend, horror and mystery associated with this wild and rugged landscape, and in particular, whatever you do, try not to let your mind dwell on The Beast.

The Beast is the result of some sixty sightings of a black panther-like big cat, supposedly three to five feet long and sporting white-yellow eyes, combined with numerous reports of mutilated livestock. The evidence was robust enough that in 1995 the government ordered an official investigation into the existence of such a beast. The report finally concluded that there was no verifiable evidence of a big cat on Bodmin Moor, although it was careful to state that there was no evidence against it, either.

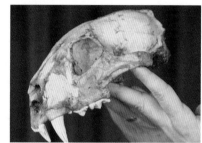

A leopard's skull

Shortly after the report was published the public were flabbergasted when a small boy found a leopard skull lying on the banks of the River Fowey. Big-cat speculation reached fever pitch. Had it escaped from a nearby zoo? Was it the author of the mutilations? The Natural History Museum, boringly, soon found the leopard skull to have been imported into this country as part of a leopardskin rug.

Could this be the Beast?

Once again, the controversy died down, although sightings were still reported with reasonable regularity, until, in 1998, video footage was released that clearly showed a black animal, probably a big cat, around three and a half feet long. The video, described by the curator of Newquay Zoo and wild-cat expert as 'the best evidence yet' that big cats do indeed roam Bodmin Moor, was part of another batch of information submitted to the government by local MP [Member of Parliament] Paul Tyler.

Theories abound. If it does exist (and many swear it does), perhaps the animal is a big cat that escaped from a zoo or a private collection and was not reported because it had been imported illegally, a hypothesis rejected by scientists on the grounds that the numbers needed to sustain a breeding population would be too large for the food supply. Some believe the animal is a species of wild cat that is thought to have become extinct in Britain more than a hundred years ago. Some, after reading reports not just of hissing and growling but of sounds like a woman screaming, are inclined to blame the paranormal. Meanwhile, the sightings continue.

You have been warned!

Exercise 3: The Beast of Bodmin

1 Using information from the passage, describe Bodmin Moor and the legendary Beast of Bodmin.

2 Explain the meaning of 'robust enough' and 'flabbergasted'.

3 According to the passage, what evidence is there that the Beast of Bodmin is real?

4 According to the passage, what are the likely explanations for the Beast of Bodmin and what have scientists and other people said about them? You should answer in your own words.

5 Write a summary of the different accounts of the Beast and the findings related to them. You should write about 100–130 words.

6 What do you think is the attitude of the Cornish Tourist Board towards the legend of the Beast of Bodmin. (Consider the last line of the extract.)

Perhaps the most famous of modern myths concerns the strange happenings associated with the Bermuda Triangle, an area of sea in the western part of the North Atlantic Ocean. Here are some details about it. Read this extract carefully and then answer the questions that follow on page 37.

Extract 4

Bermuda Triangle: Behind the Intrigue

BY HILLARY MAYELL

On a sunny day 58 years ago, five Navy planes took off from their base in Florida on a routine training mission, known as Flight 19. Neither the planes nor the crew were ever seen again.

Thus was a legend born. The Bermuda Triangle is an area roughly bounded by Miami, Bermuda, and Puerto Rico. No one keeps statistics, but in the last century, numerous ships and planes have simply vanished without a trace within the imaginary triangle.

Unusual features of the area had been noted in the past. Christopher Columbus wrote in his log about bizarre compass bearings in the area. But the region didn't get its name until August 1964, when Vincent Gaddis coined the term 'Bermuda Triangle' in a cover story for *Argosy* magazine about the disappearance of Flight 19. The article stimulated a virtual cottage industry in myth-making.

‖▶

Many exotic theories have been propounded to explain what happened to the missing travellers.

The disappearances have been attributed to the machinations of enormous sea monsters, giant squid, or extra-terrestrials. Alien abductions, the existence of a mysterious third dimension created by unknown beings, and ocean flatulence – the ocean suddenly spewing great quantities of trapped methane – have all been suggested as culprits.

The reality, say many, is far more prosaic. They argue that a sometimes treacherous Mother Nature, human error, shoddy craftsmanship or design, and just plain bad luck can explain the many disappearances.

'The region is highly travelled and has been a busy crossroads since the early days of European exploration,' said John Reilly, a historian with the US Naval Historical Foundation. 'To say quite a few ships and airplanes have gone down there is like saying there are an awful lot of car accidents on the New Jersey Turnpike – surprise, surprise.'

Lieutenant A.L. Russell, in the US Coast Guard's official response to Bermuda Triangle inquiries, writes: 'It has been our experience that the combined forces of nature and the unpredictability of mankind outdo science-fiction stories many times each year.'

Graveyard of the Atlantic

The Bermuda Triangle region has some unusual features. It's one of only two places on Earth – the other being an area nicknamed the Devil's Sea off the east coast of Japan, which has a similar mysterious reputation – where true north and magnetic north line up, which could make compass readings dicey.

It is also home to some of the deepest underwater trenches in the world; wreckage could settle in a watery grave miles below the surface of the ocean. Most of the sea floor in the Bermuda Triangle is about 19 000 feet

(5800 metres) down; near its southern tip, the Puerto Rico Trench dips at one point to 27 500 feet (8230 metres) below sea level.

Treacherous shoals and reefs can be found along the continental shelf. Strong currents over the reefs constantly breed new navigational hazards, according to the Coast Guard.

Then there's the weather.

'The biggest issues in that area normally are hurricanes, but it's not particularly a spawning area for storms,' said Dave Feit, chief of the marine forecast branch of the National Oceanic and Atmospheric Administration's Marine Prediction Center.

However, Feit pointed out, the Gulf Stream travels along the western edge of the triangle and could be a factor. The Gulf Stream is like a 40- to 50-mile-wide (64- to 80-kilometre-wide) river within the ocean that circulates in the North Atlantic Ocean. The warm water and two- to four-knot currents can create weather patterns that remain channelled within it.

'If you have the right atmospheric conditions, you could get quite unexpectedly high waves,' said Feit. 'If wave heights are 8 feet (2.4 metres) outside of the Gulf Stream, they could be two or even three times higher within it. Sailors can sometimes identify the Gulf Stream by the clouds and thunderstorms over it.'

The Coast Guard also notes that unpredictable Caribbean-Atlantic storms can yield waterspouts that often spell disaster for pilots and mariners.

Still, given a choice between the horrifying idea of a giant squid's tentacles wrestling an innocent ship to the sea floor, or an alien abduction, versus human error, shoddy engineering, and a temperamental Mother Nature – who could resist the legend of the Bermuda Triangle?

Exercise 4: Bermuda Triangle

1 By referring to the opening paragraphs, explain, using your own words, what the mystery of the Bermuda Triangle is.
2 Explain what is meant by 'a virtual cottage industry in myth-making'.
3 Using your own words, explain what theories have been put forward to explain the disappearances in the Bermuda Triangle, and how other people have answered these theories.
4 Explain, using your own words, the comments made by John Reilly and Lieutenant Russell at the end of the first section of this passage.
5 From the 'Graveyard of the Atlantic' section, write a summary of what you have learnt about the unusual features of the Bermuda Triangle. You should write about 180–200 words.

Reading for pleasure

Here is a retelling of the story of Rama and Sita, an ancient Hindu myth from Northern India.

Rama and Sita

This is a story about Prince Rama, the great warrior, who was married to the beautiful Sita. Rama and Sita were really gods in human form.

Prince Rama was meant to take over the throne from his father the king, but his wicked stepmother had tricked his father into sending him away into the forest. With him went his wife, Sita. Rama had begged Sita to stay safely in the palace while he was in the forest, but she declared it was a thousand times better to be in the forest with Rama than in the richest palace without him.

So Rama and Sita went to live in the forest together. They lived a simple, peaceful life in a small cottage.

But, before long, their peace was disturbed. One day, Sita was spotted by the demon king, Ravana. Of all the demons who lived in the forest, Ravana was the most terrible. He had twenty arms and ten heads, with eyes as red as coal fires and a mouthful of yellow fangs. When Ravana saw the beautiful Sita, he immediately came up with a plan to kidnap her and make her his wife.

One day, when Rama and Sita were walking in the forest, they saw the most beautiful deer you can imagine. Its golden hide was as bright as the sun, its silver antlers as bright as the moon, its hooves shone as black as night, and its eyes were as blue as sapphires.

So delighted was Sita when she saw the deer that she begged Rama to catch it for her. Rama was worried that this was some demon trick to try and split them up, but Sita pleaded with Rama, until he agreed to try and catch the deer for her.

As soon as Sita was alone, the demon Ravana swooped down and swept Sita up into his chariot pulled by winged monsters. Despite her terror Sita thought quickly and scattered her jewellery piece by piece – first her golden anklets, then her earrings, then her glittering scarf – as a trail for Rama to follow. Far below a white monkey looked up and, seeing the glittering jewellery, thought the stars were falling.

In the midst of the forest, Rama tracked down the beautiful deer. But when he caught hold of it, the deer changed into a terrible demon that broke away from Rama's grasp and flew into the sky. Realising that he had been tricked, Prince Rama ran back to the cottage as fast as he could, his heart filled with dread. Finding Sita gone, he searched frantically until he came upon the trail of jewellery that Sita had left.

Rama followed this golden trail until he met Hanuman, the white monkey, who had seen Sita's jewellery fall from the sky. Hanuman was a very special monkey because he was the monkey king. Hanuman took Rama to the monkey city that lay under the hills in a giant cave. All the monkeys of the city were called to the marble square in the centre of the city, and messages were sent out to monkeys all over the world. They came in their millions from the woods and caves, and with them came their friends the bears. Twenty-three million animals filled the city and covered the hills like a great shaggy sea. After they had heard what had happened, they spread out to search the world for Sita.

It was the monkey Hanuman who came to the island where Sita was being held prisoner. The monkeys and bears with him stared in despair at the giant crashing waves that surrounded the island, but Hanuman, the son of the wind god, climbed to the highest hill, took a mighty breath and leapt into the clouds, and over the crashing waves. He landed on the island and quickly found Sita in a grove of trees near the palace. There she sat refusing to marry the evil Ravana.

Sita was overjoyed when she found out who Hanuman was and she gave him a pearl from her hair to take to Rama. Then, Hanuman bounded away to fetch Rama and the great army of monkeys and bears.

But still the giant ocean waves kept Rama and his army away from the island. And so the army began to build a bridge of rocks and grass and sand.

The squirrels came running out of the woods to help, every animal – large and small – contributed to the building, and soon the bridge stretched a hundred miles to the island, and the animals poured across their bridge.

Long and terrible was the battle, as the animals fought the evil demons. Many great deeds were done, until at last Rama faced the demon Ravana on the battlefield. With his arrows Rama struck again and again at the heads of Ravana, but each time he chopped one off with his sword a new one grew.

Then Rama took up his special bow and arrow that had been made by the sky god. He chanted a special prayer and shot. The gods of wind and fire guided the arrow and it pierced Ravana's chest in a blinding flash. Ravana fell dead in an instant.

The entire world rejoiced. The reign of the demons was over and Rama and Sita returned to their own country to rule. In celebration, the gods showered flowers from the sky, and the people lined the streets with flags and garlands. In every home, an oil lamp was put in the window to welcome back Rama and Sita and their great army. They ruled happily for many years until it was time for them to leave their life on earth and return to heaven.

An effigy of Ravana is burnt at the Hindu festival of Divali

For Hindus, this story shows how good will always triumph over evil in the same way as a little oil lamp will destroy total darkness.

Writing

Activity

Write your own contemporary legend set in your own school or community. The story could be totally made up or be based on actual events that have occurred recently.

Extended activity

As you have seen from the examples on pages 30–39, myths and legends are a feature of all societies and they are still being created today. There are almost certainly myths and legends associated with your own country and quite possibly with the particular area in which you live.

||||➡

> 1 Working in small groups, research the myths and legends that are local to you – some members of the group could explore ancient myths and others look at contemporary ones. If you have the resources available, you might also want to investigate whether the stories you have found relating to your country have similarities to those found in other parts of the world.
> 2 Now rewrite the stories and collect them together in a booklet or loose-leaf folder.

Speaking and listening

Activity

In your group, present a dramatised reading of one of the myths or legends relating to your local area that you have researched.

Key skills

Vocabulary and spelling

Suffixes

A **suffix** is a letter or group of letters added to the end of a word (or a word stem) in order to form a new word or to alter the grammatical function of the original word.

For example, adding the suffix *–ness* to the stem of the adjective *heavy* creates the noun *heaviness*. (Notice that when the suffix is added, the *y* at the end of the original word changes to an *i*. This is a spelling rule to remember for all other similar words.)

The main function of suffixes is to create new nouns, verbs and adjectives. Here is a list of the most common suffixes in English:

Noun suffixes	Examples	Original word
–acy	privacy, numeracy	private, numerate (adjectives)
–al	proposal	propose (verb)
–ance, –ence	maintenance, evidence	maintain (verb), evident (adjective)
–dom	freedom, officialdom	free (adjective), official (noun)
–er, –or	shopper, protector	shop, protect (verbs)
–ism	absolutism	absolute (adjective)

–ist	saxophonist	saxophone (noun)
–ity, –ty	humidity	humid (adjective)
–ment	argument	argue (verb)
–ness	heaviness	heavy (adjective)
–ship	relationship	relation (noun)
–sion, –tion	recession, abbreviation	recede, abbreviate (verbs)
Verb suffixes	**Examples**	**Original word**
–ate	irritate	irritation (noun)
–en	cheapen	cheap (adjective)
–ify, –fy	horrify	horror (noun)
–ise, –ize	civilise	civil (adjective)
Adjective suffixes	**Examples**	**Original word**
–able, –ible	lovable, accessible	love (verb), access (noun)
–al	regional	region (noun)
–esque	picturesque	picture (noun)
–ful	plentiful	plenty (noun)
–ic, –ical	mythic, biological	myth, biology (nouns)
–ious, –ous	atrocious, portentous	atrocity, portent (nouns)
–ish	devilish	devil (noun)
–ive	active	act (verb)
–less	hopeless	hope (noun)
–y	lazy	laze (verb)

Exercise: Finding words ending in suffixes

By referring to a dictionary or by researching online (using websites such as FindTheWord.info) make a list of other words ending with the suffixes in the table. As you do so, try to find common links between them – for example, most words ending in *–ship* are likely to be abstract nouns. Be careful, however, as words ending with the same group of letters are not necessarily all formed by the addition of a suffix. The *–ist* at the end of *saxophonist* is a suffix, but the last three letters of *twist* are not, for example.

Confusions

Using the wrong form of a suffix is one of the most common causes of spelling errors in English, in particular through the confusion of *–ance/–ence*, *–ense/–ence* or *–able/–ible*.

Exercise: Using the correct suffix

Copy the word stems that follow and add what you think is the correct ending. When you have finished, check your spellings in a dictionary and try to remember the correct form of any words that you spelt incorrectly.

1 Add *–ance* or *–ence* to:

abund–	dilig–	guid–
assist–	eloqu–	nuis–
correspond–	exist–	rever–

2 Add *–ense* or *–ence* to:

abs–	imm–	pret–
disp–	int–	recomp–
exp–	off–	

3 Add *–able* or *–ible* to:

advis–	illeg–	laud–
contempt–	incorrig–	respons–
cred–	indefens–	sens–
ed–	indispens–	vis–
forc–	inexhaust–	

English usage

Plurals

Another cause of confusion for people learning to express themselves in English is how to form the plurals of nouns. Here is a list of the main ways in which nouns in English change from singular to plural:

- The most common way of forming the plural of a noun is by adding *–s* to the singular form: *book – books*; *house – houses*.
- Sometimes the plural is formed by adding *–es*: *dress – dresses*; *tomato – tomatoes*; *potato – potatoes*.
- Less common, but worth remembering, is adding *–en* to the singular form: *ox – oxen*; *child – children*; *brother – brethren*.
- The *–y* at the end of the singular form may change to *–ies*: *lady – ladies*; *baby – babies*.
- The *–fe* at the end of the singular may change to *–ves*: *wife – wives*; *knife – knives*.
- Vowels in the middle of the singular form may change: *goose – geese*; *mouse – mice*.
- Some words do not change at all between singular and plural: *sheep*; *deer*; *species*; *salmon*.
- Some words which have entered English from other languages have kept their plural form in the original language: *addendum – addenda*; *crisis – crises*; *formula – formulae*; *phenomenon – phenomena*.
- Some imported foreign words have adopted English plural forms: *octopus – octopuses*; *syllabus – syllabuses*.

Comparison of adjectives

Most adjectives and adverbs in English have three stages of comparison: **positive**, **comparative** and **superlative**:

- **Positive:** This is the standard form of the adjective or adverb: *good, happy, quickly*.
- **Comparative:** This is the form used to show comparison: *better, happier, more quickly*.
- **Superlative:** This is the form that expresses perfection: *best, happiest, most quickly*.

Note that most adverbs take the words *more* and *most* before their comparative and superlative forms; for example, *more quickly* and *most quickly*, not *quicklier* and *quickliest*! However, *fast* is an exception to this rule: *faster, fastest*.

With adjectives, the situation is less definite. Many have comparatives and superlatives formed by adding *–er* and *–est* to the normal, positive form; others, such as *beautiful*, form their comparatives and superlatives with *more* and *most*. As a general rule, the more syllables there are in the positive form of the adjective, the more likely it is that *more* and *most* will be used.

Be warned:

- If a comparison is being made between *two* people or things, then the *comparative* form of the adjective should be used; for example, *Helena and Ravi compared their pencils; Helena's was sharper* [not *sharpest*]. However, if three or more people are involved in the comparison, then the superlative form should be used; for example, *Ravi's maths homework was the best in the class*.
- Some adjectives exist only in their positive form – *unique* means 'the only one of its kind' and so it is grammatically incorrect to describe something as *more unique* or *most unique*. Similarly, *excellent* means 'the best that can be achieved' and does not have a comparative or superlative form.

Reading

Leaflets

Leaflets are small, pocket-sized printed documents that aim to provide basic information about an attraction or a campaign in an easily assimilable form – a form easy to understand or take in. They consist of not only words but also diagrams and illustrations intended to convey details clearly to readers. It is very likely that your school produces leaflets on various policies to provide information for parents when they visit the school; it is also likely that you have read a range of leaflets about places to visit on holiday. Indeed, some of you may well have built up your own collection of leaflets on places you have visited over the years.

You will find three examples of leaflets on pages 44–51. The first, the Rocky Springs Park leaflet shown on this and the next two pages, was written in the 1970s. It gives details of a theme park in the USA which closed in 1981. Read through it carefully and then answer the questions that follow on page 47.

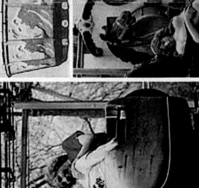

The Carousel, an antique fantasy of exotic animals, glowing with the love an old German master put into each hand carved piece. Wild or tame, there are over a dozen more rides to suit your appetite. And the kids have a land all their own, a playground loaded with swings and things and rides just their size - from Ferris Wheels to Flying Swans.

So many things to do at Rocky Springs.... grab a canoe and drift along the lazy Conestoga River. Bean a birdie, bag a bunnie and win yourself a giant moose (stuffed of course) at our games of skill. Watch craftsmen perform their art, beat the electronic games in our big arcade, be a pinball wizard or skeeball star · rollerskate, disco, bingo!

Take a giant step back... to simpler days and lemonade prices. We're one of America's oldest amusement parks, entertaining you in a style that's ours alone.

We've restored our collection of magnificent old rides and added new ones. Our 45 acres of lush woodland hold a full day of rides, shows and excitement. It all adds up to the kind of magical, carefree, good-time family fun your grandparents laughed with and 'loved long, long ago.

Rocky Springs is excitement!
Roll like thunder on the Whirling Dervish, whirl like a leaf in the wind. Hurtle, darting and diving, on a breathtaking journey with our racy rodent, The Wild Mouse. Or ride the Cuddle-up, the fastest in the country; spin and careen as the world flashes by and dancing strobes dazzle the night.
Do you like your excitement a touch on the tame side? There's the Laugh in the Dark, a suspenseful journey through a world of surprises · just made for hugging.

Enjoy a parade, a magic show, or a thumping oompah band.
The fun goes on after dark as the park comes ablaze with the color and magic of thousands of lights.

Come, tie a balloon to your wrist, sample a double-dip mocha rum ice cream cone and make friends with the child who lives on inside each of us.
Rocky Springs Park...we're a lot of good fun.

Rocky Springs Park

More fun for your money.

Yesteryear at Rocky.

Rocky Springs Park began in the early 1880's as a bathing resort. A stern-paddle steamboat, the Lady Gay, ferried passengers to the park, which was little more than a cleared beach and pavillions for dancing. Within ten years, Rocky Springs grew into one of the nation's first amusement parks. A fleet of steamboats navigated the Conestoga River until after the turn of the century. The nation's first ice cream cones were manufactured at the park in 1904. One of America's earliest rollercoasters, the Figure Eight Toboggan Slide, delighted the adventuresome. And legendary figures like Jack Dempsey, Rudee Vallee, and Carrie Nation entertained capacity audiences at Rocky Springs' 2,000 seat theatre, for some years the largest theatre in the east.

It's easy to relive the fun of the past at Rocky Springs Park. Many of our rides, buildings, and attractions are much the same as they were three generations ago. And our history is displayed in words and old photographs around the park./

Roads to Rocky.

Rocky Springs Park is located on Millport Road (South Duke Street extended), two miles southeast of Lancaster city.

From Rt. 30: West on Rt. 462 to third traffic light, then south (left turn) on Lampeter Road. Continue one mile, turn right onto Millport Road. Rocky Springs Park is one-half mile on right.

From Rts. 283, 222, 272, 72 and 501: Take bypass (Rt. 30 & 283) east to Hempstead Road exit. Turn right, cross overpass, then make immediate left onto Greenfield Road. At T intersection, turn left onto Pitney Road. Continue two miles and follow signs.

From Lancaster city: Follow South Duke Street two miles to just past the Lancaster County Park. Rocky Springs is on the left.

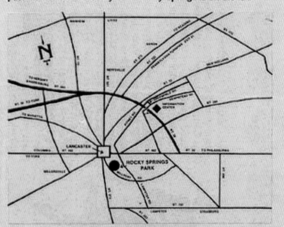

General Information

Set in the rolling, wooded hills bordering the Conestoga River just beyond the Lancaster city limits, Rocky Springs Park offers rides, games, delicious food, shows and special events, canoeing, bingo, dancing, rollerskating and picnicing.

Pavillions and catering are available for groups of 25 to 1000. Discounts vary with the size of your group. For more information contact: Group Sales Office, Rocky Springs Park, 1441 Millport Rd., Lancaster, Pa. 17602, or phone (717) 291-5913.

General Admission: $4.50. Includes tickets good for rides and food. Children under three years of age admitted free.

Open 10 A.M. to 10 P.M. daily May 26 through Labor Day; 10 A.M. to 8 P.M. weekends September 8 through November 4.

Rocky Springs Park

1441 Millport Road, Lancaster, PA.

The Rocky Springs leaflet was folded into three. The front of the leaflet is shown on page 44 and the inside on page 45. The sections above were at the back of the leaflet

Exercise 1: Rocky Springs Park

1 Give the names of three of the attractions that you could find at Rocky Springs Park.

2 If you did not greatly enjoy scary rides, which ride(s) would you have found most suitable?

3 What other entertainments could you find at Rocky Springs Park as well as the rides?

4 Give examples from the leaflet that show that Rocky Springs Park was deliberately setting out to appeal to visitors' nostalgia for earlier times.

5 When was Rocky Springs Park first opened and what was its original function?

6 What evidence can you find in the leaflet that suggests that the Park was popular in its earlier days?

7 How do the photographs of the various activities help to reinforce the points made in the text of the leaflet?

8 Look up 'careen' in a dictionary and give its meaning as used in the leaflet.

9 How far does the Park cater for the interests of the whole family (grandparents, parents and children)? Give examples of activities that would appeal to all age groups.

10 At the end of the leaflet is the statement, 'Rocky Springs Park ... we're a lot of good fun.' How far do you think this sums up the information contained in the leaflet? Do you think the leaflet would be more successful if it contained more dynamic language? Give your reasons. Try to find an example of a more recent leaflet for a similar attraction and compare this with the one for Rocky Springs Park.

The two leaflets that follow are intended to serve slightly different purposes than the one for Rocky Springs Park. 'Got a Teenager?' (on pages 48–49) has been produced by an organisation called Parentline and 'Death Valley Eggs' (on pages 50–51) is from an organisation called Animal Aid.

Read both leaflets carefully and then do the exercise on page 50.

The front and back covers of the 'Got a Teenager?' leaflet. The image on page 49 shows the two inside pages

WHAT YOU CAN DO

Sometimes the things that your teenager says may hurt you. They seem to have changed from the cooperative child you once knew. But remember they are growing up to be young adults. They need to learn how to think and act for themselves but most of all they need your love, help and advice to make sense of it all.

◑ Parentline Plus tips

☑ Keep an open mind and listen to their point of view.

☑ Change the way you talk to them. Rather than nagging, just chat when you get the opportunity such as before they go to their room, or after watching TV.

☑ Agree boundaries with all those involved in bringing up your children. Knowing there are rules helps your teenagers feel safe and secure.

☑ Understand why they may be behaving badly. They may be moody or have 'attitude' because they find it hard to put their worries into words.

☑ Compromise. Sometimes it is worth meeting them half way. It shows you have listened to them.

☑ Start to give them some responsibility for their own safety but make sure you have discussed the best ways to keep safe first.

☑ Enjoy your teenager as a young adult and let them know when you are proud of them.

SETTING LIMITS

Boundaries are about setting the bottom line. They show what you value, and what's right for you and your family. They are the principles that guide you and help you to keep your child safe and secure. Teenagers will often test the limits you have set them – it's part of growing up.

◑ Parentline Plus tips

☑ Tell your children clearly what you want and why, and listen to their point of view. Boundaries work far better if they are made and agreed by everyone.

☑ Make a compromise. It doesn't mean you're giving in but shows that you value their opinions and are letting your children take more responsibility for themselves.

☑ Trust them. Children are far more likely to cooperate if they feel trusted and part of a team.

☑ Give your teenagers some responsibility for their own safety as they get older. Give them ideas about how they can keep themselves safe.

☑ If it's not working talk over why not and make a new rule or agreement together. Be prepared to talk about or change the boundaries right through the teenage years as your children grow and mature.

→ **NEW WEBSITE**
www.gotateenager.org.uk

Parentline Plus has just launched a brand new social networking website for parents of teenagers. Whether you are worried about drugs and unsafe sex or just can't seem to get through the day without a row, then you are not alone. Meet other parents online and share the challenges and successes of parenting your child through the teenage years. Features include message boards, e-learning modules, interactive TV shows for parents and much more....

The front of the 'Death Valley Eggs' leaflet (reduced in size). The image on page 51 shows the inside

Exercise 2: 'Got a Teenager?' and 'Death Valley Eggs'

Write a detailed comparison of the two leaflets 'Got a Teenager?' and 'Death Valley Eggs' in which you look at the similarities and differences between them. Make sure that you support your comments by referring to and quoting from the content of the leaflets. For each leaflet, you should consider the following points in particular:

- the purpose of the leaflet
- its audience – who it is aimed at
- the information it contains
- its layout – for example, the use of illustrations, colour, subheadings, different fonts
- the tone of the language – in particular, the use of emotive vocabulary and the ways in which facts and opinions are conveyed to readers
- how successful the leaflet is in achieving its purpose; give your reasons.

Writing

Activity

This is your opportunity to produce a leaflet of your own. Here are some possible subjects:

- a leaflet aimed at new students coming to your school. Rather than producing an 'official' type of leaflet (similar to one giving information for parents), you could produce an 'alternative' guide to the school and how to cope with the first few weeks, written from a student's perspective and aimed at other students ▐▐▐▶

There are approximately 30 million egg-laying hens in the UK. Around 75% are kept in battery cages. The others are kept in 'alternative' systems such as 'barn' or 'free range'. But look at these photos. Is there really much difference?

A recently-rescued free range hen

Photo: FAWN

BATTERY HELL

In battery units, four or five hens are crammed into a space not much bigger than a microwave oven. They are barely able to move, let alone stretch their wings. Battery cages are so inhumane that they will be banned in the EU from 2012 – but that means years of suffering ahead. And the replacement, so-called 'enriched' cages, will make little difference – because a cage is still a cage and the extra space the hens will have is equivalent to the size of a postcard.

Photo: Viva!

BARN MISERY

The term 'barn eggs' is used deliberately to dupe the public into thinking that the hens are kept in bright, airy conditions with fresh straw on the floor. Not true! Though uncaged, the hens are still confined to dirty, overcrowded sheds. They will never see daylight, breathe fresh air or be able to exercise their natural instincts.

Photo: FAWN

FREE RANGE?

Many people associate 'free range' with 'cruelty-free' and assume the hens live a natural life. The reality is very different: thousands of 'free range' hens may be packed into huge sheds with limited access to the outdoors. Often, less than half of the birds roam freely into and out of the sheds because the others are simply unable to fight their way through to the exits.

MALE CHICKS KILLED

Each year in the UK, approximately 30 million day-old male chicks are gassed or tossed alive into giant industrial shredders, 'disposed of' because they are unable to lay eggs and are considered too scrawny a type of chicken for meat production.

NOT ALL THEY'RE CRACKED UP TO BE

Eggs contain saturated fat, one of the main causes of heart disease – and they are among the highest sources of dietary cholesterol. Research also indicates that eggs can inhibit the absorption of iron (needed for healthy blood, cells and nerves) and contribute to loss of calcium (necessary for healthy bones). There are no nutrients in eggs that cannot be obtained from other foods. Cutting out animal products entirely is the *really* healthy option.

Send for a free recipe pack. See reverse.

Tel 01732 364546　　　**ANIMAL AID**　　　www.animalaid.org.uk

> - a leaflet aimed at raising people's awareness of an important issue (for example, the need to look after your local environment, the importance of eating healthily). Think carefully about the audience for this leaflet – will it be for your peers (people your age) or for people of an older or younger generation?
> - a leaflet intended for visitors to your local area, making them aware of places, facilities and amenities that may be of interest to them during their visit.
>
> Producing these leaflets is an opportunity to make use of the ICT facilities available to you and to work in small groups to produce a professional-looking leaflet.

Reading

Reports

Here are two reports that deal with the same subject. Read both reports carefully and then answer the question on page 54.

Report 1

New Year Fun

Dear Headteacher

We're in class 8G and we all thought that it would be a great idea if we could organise a charity fund-raising activity. So we had a discussion and Lee (or at least, I think it was Lee but it could have been Soraya) came up with the idea that we ought to organise a New Year celebration party for the kids in the local Under 5s Playgroup. So we made arrangements with the people who run it and decided on what we would charge for admission then we all thought about what we could each do.

Anyway, all of our class arrived at the playgroup on New Year's Day and started to get things ready. We had some food and drink that we'd organised and we had some play equipment and other things that we thought we'd do, like some of the class had brought along hi-fi equipment so that there could be dancing and just after we'd got things ready it was time to start so we opened the doors and loads of little kids along with their parents came rushing in.

We didn't charge anything for admission but they had to pay to buy food and to take part in the activities. The trouble was they all wanted to do everything at once and none of them had the right money so it was hard to give them change and then the Bouncy Castle collapsed because too many of them were climbing on it at once and we hadn't got enough food ready and so some of the young kids started crying because they thought they wouldn't get any but eventually we got some more sandwiches and cakes and hot dogs ready and then they were happy again but it really was very chaotic at times but in the end they all went home happy and although we had a lot of clearing up to do, we were happy as well because we'd made a lot of money for charity.

Report 2

Report on Charity Activity

To: Headteacher, Green Trees Secondary School

From: Class 8G, Green Trees Secondary School

Background

In order to raise money for the Children in Need charity members of Class 8G at Green Trees Secondary School arranged a New Year's Day party for the Tiny Tots Playgroup for Under 5s. The event was held at the Tiny Tots Centre in President Road from 14.00 to 16.00 hrs on 1 January.

All 26 members of Class 8G were involved and between them had organised refreshments and a range of activities suitable for the under-5 age group.

Details of the Event

A large number of children from the playgroup, accompanied by their parents, attended the event. Those members of Class 8G who were supervising admission counted between 60 and 67 children attending. (Owing to the large number present at the start of the event and the fact that no admission charge was made, it was not possible for an exact count to be made.)

All of the activities and stalls provided at the event proved to be very popular with the children from the playgroup and at the end of the afternoon all the food and drink provided for them had been consumed. The large number of children present at one time caused some problems – at one stage food ran out and there was a delay before a second round was produced. Also, there was a malfunction with the Bouncy Castle as a result of overcrowding and there were also some problems with providing change at some of the stalls. However, all these problems were eventually dealt with without affecting the enjoyment of those attending.

After the event had finished, Class 8G stayed behind to clear up the hall in which the event was held. In total, a profit of 377 euros was made which will be donated to the Children in Need charity organisation.

Recommendations

Although the event was successful, some points arose which should be kept in mind for any future, similar activities. The key recommendations are:

• It is important that an exact count is made of how many people are present and so it is suggested that in future tickets should be issued in advance and handed in when visitors arrive. Accurate advance information as to the number of people likely to be present will also help in planning the amount of food needed and prevent a shortage occurring as happened this year.

- More careful supervision should be kept on activities such as the Bouncy Castle. In future, strict control should be kept over the number of children allowed on the activity at any one time.

- All those running stalls and other activities should be provided with a 'float' of small change before the event opens to ensure that there are no problems in dealing with visitors who do not have the exact amount of money required.

Exercise 3: Reports 1 and 2

If you were the headteacher who received these reports, which would you find the more informative and why? Decide which report is less effective and then write a brief commentary on it (about 200–250 words) in which you point out particular examples of why it is not effective and give your reasons for saying so.

Writing

Writing reports is almost certainly something that you will have to do not only during your time at school, but also in your adult, working life. As with everything you write, it is important that you have a clear idea of both the purpose of the report (why you are writing it) and the audience for whom you are producing it (who will read it). When writing a report, you should pay close attention to the following advice:

- The person who is reading your report is likely to be very busy and so information should be conveyed clearly and accurately; your main concern should be to communicate the main points directly and without any unnecessary details or digressions.

- Details should be accurate and precise; do not make vague or uncertain generalisations.

- The report should be written factually and in an objective tone. It should not include personal emotions or opinions.

- Be concise but also include all essential details. Remember, there is an important difference between brevity and conciseness: you can make a report short by leaving out key points, but it will not be a very effective report if you do so! You can, however, make your report concise by leaving out unnecessary words such as 'each and every one', 'during the course of events', and so on.

- If it is necessary to make recommendations as a result of the report, then they should be clearly based on details in the report and be practicable, manageable and positive.

Activity

Keeping in mind the advice given on page 54, write a report on **one** of the following:

- While taking part in a playground activity at school, you and your friends accidentally broke a classroom window. Write a report for your form teacher in which you explain clearly, concisely and honestly exactly how the accident occurred.
- You are looking for some part-time work and have recently visited a company where you hope to be employed. Write a report for your careers teacher at school giving details of what the company does, what work you have applied to do there and what is involved, how many hours a week you will work and how you intend to organise this so that your school work will not be affected.

Reading

Historical and cultural contexts

Earlier in this chapter we looked at a publicity leaflet for the Rocky Springs Park which was printed in the 1970s. If you had not been given that information, you would most probably have thought that it was a rather unexciting leaflet and perhaps that this was because it looked rather old fashioned. However, had you been a teenager in the 1970s you would have had a totally different response to the leaflet as you would have read it in the context of other leaflets printed at the same time, just as although nowadays the attractions offered by the Park may seem rather dated and quaint, 40 years ago they were very much state of the art.

When we read any work of imaginative literature, such as a novel or a poem, we first of all approach it with the beliefs and values of our own society at the front of our minds. This is understandable and there are some values (such as showing respect to older people or respecting other people's lives and property) that have been common to all civilised societies throughout history. However, we should not assume that the world in which the characters in a novel exist is exactly the same as the world we live in.

If we are reading a historical novel set in the sixteenth century, we do not expect the characters to use mobile phones. The author will have created the world of the past for us and we take the setting into account when we read the story – we expect the author to be consistent in writing about the world in which his/her characters are placed. An **anachronism** is the name given to an error when an author includes something from the wrong period of time; for example, having sixteenth-century characters using mobile phones. Even the greatest authors are sometimes guilty of this – in *Julius Caesar* Shakespeare has a clock striking in ancient Rome although, in fact, striking clocks were not invented until at least a thousand years after the events described in his play.

Things become a little more difficult when we are reading books written by authors who lived during a different period of time to our own. Sixteenth-century authors writing about the world with which they were familiar had no reason to explain how it differed from the twenty-first century – even if they could imagine what life today would be like.

So, when we read books written either in an earlier period of time or in a country which has different social and religious values from those with which we are familiar, we need to take into account the historical and cultural context in order to understand fully the behaviour and attitudes of the characters involved.

For example, in the medieval period, everyone believed that the Sun, Moon and stars orbited the Earth and that the Earth was the centre of the universe. Many people also believed that the stars influenced people's characters and their destinies. When we read the poetry of Chaucer (*c.*1340–1400) we need to keep this view of the world clearly in our minds in order to understand why his characters think and act as they do. Similarly, when we read stories by present-day African writers it is important that we have some awareness of the cultural values of the society about which they are writing, such as its respect for the old tribal beliefs and traditions (shown in Chinua Achebe's story 'Dead Men's Path', in *Student's Book 1*, for example).

Although we need to be aware of the historical and social contexts in order to appreciate fully books written in a different period of time or by authors living in different cultures from our own, this does not mean that these books can be enjoyed only for what they tell us about past times or different countries. One of the main reasons that good literature appeals to readers no matter where or when they live is because the characters are driven by emotions which are common to all humans. Chaucer's characters are just as greedy and dishonest or noble and well intentioned as those in Achebe's stories or the people who are your neighbours in real life. These universal truths about human nature are what give literature its appeal, but an understanding of the world in which characters live certainly helps to enrich that appeal!

The two extracts that follow have very different historical and social contexts. The first is from Shakespeare's play *Romeo and Juliet* and the second from a short story by the contemporary writer Ruth Prawer Jhabvala. The play reflects some social and historical attitudes of the time in which it was written whereas the story makes some points about the difficulties experienced by a European girl marrying into a different culture to her own.

Read the following extract carefully and then answer the question on pages 59–60.

Romeo and Juliet

In this extract from the play, 14-year-old Juliet has secretly married Romeo, who has been banished for killing her cousin Tybalt in a swordfight. Unaware that their daughter is married, her parents, Lord and Lady Capulet, have arranged a marriage for Juliet to the rich Count Paris. In this scene (which has been slightly edited) Juliet is informed that the arranged marriage will take place very soon. Near the end of the extract, some words printed in italics are explained for you to the right of the text.

Lady Capulet:	Well, well, thou hast a careful father, child; One who, to put thee from thy heaviness, Hath sorted out a sudden day of joy, That thou expect'st not nor I look'd not for.
Juliet:	Madam, in happy time, what day is that?
Lady Capulet:	Marry, my child, early next Thursday morn, The gallant, young and noble gentleman, The County Paris, at Saint Peter's Church, Shall happily make thee there a joyful bride.
Juliet:	Now, by Saint Peter's Church and Peter too, He shall not make me there a joyful bride. I wonder at this haste; that I must wed Ere he, that should be husband, comes to woo. I pray you, tell my lord and father, madam, I will not marry yet; and, when I do, I swear, It shall be Romeo, whom you know I hate, Rather than Paris. These are news indeed!
Lady Capulet:	Here comes your father; tell him so yourself, And see how he will take it at your hands.

Enter Capulet and Nurse.   ‖➡

Capulet:	When the sun sets, the air doth drizzle dew; But for the sunset of my brother's son It rains downright. How now! a conduit, girl? what, still in tears? Evermore showering? In one little body Thou counterfeit'st a bark, a sea, a wind; For still thy eyes, which I may call the sea, Do ebb and flow with tears; the bark thy body is, Sailing in this salt flood; the winds, thy sighs; Who, raging with thy tears, and they with them, Without a sudden calm, will overset Thy tempest-tossed body. How now, wife! Have you deliver'd to her our decree?
Lady Capulet:	Ay, sir; but she will none, she gives you thanks. I would the fool were married to her grave!
Capulet:	Soft! take me with you, take me with you, wife. How! will she none? doth she not give us thanks? Is she not proud? doth she not count her blest, Unworthy as she is, that we have wrought So worthy a gentleman to be her bridegroom?
Juliet:	Good father, I beseech you on my knees, Hear me with patience but to speak a word.
Capulet:	Hang thee, young baggage! disobedient wretch! I tell thee what: get thee to church o' Thursday, Or never after look me in the face: Speak not, reply not, do not answer me; My fingers itch.

Lady Capulet:	You are too hot.
Capulet:	God's bread! it makes me mad:

Day, night, hour, tide, time, work, play,
Alone, in company, still my care hath been
To have her *match'd*: and having now provided   married
A gentleman of noble parentage,
Of fair *demesnes*, youthful, and nobly train'd,   property
Stuff'd, as they say, with honourable parts,
Proportion'd as one's thought would wish a man;
And then to have a wretched *puling* fool,   whimpering
A whining *mammet*, in her fortune's tender,   doll
To answer 'I'll not wed; I cannot love,
I am too young; I pray you, pardon me.'
But, as you will not wed, I'll pardon you:
Graze where you will you shall not house with me:
Look to't, think on't, I do not use to jest.
Thursday is near; lay hand on heart, advise:
An you be mine, I'll give you to my friend;
And you be not, hang, beg, starve, die in the streets,
For, by my soul, I'll ne'er acknowledge thee,
Nor what is mine shall never do thee good:
Trust to't, bethink you; I'll not *be forsworn*.   break my
    word

Exit.

Juliet:	Is there no pity sitting in the clouds,

That sees into the bottom of my grief?
O, sweet my mother, cast me not away!
Delay this marriage for a month, a week;
Or, if you do not, make the bridal bed
In that dim monument where Tybalt lies.

Lady Capulet:	Talk not to me, for I'll not speak a word:
	Do as thou wilt, for I have done with thee.

Exercise 4: Romeo and Juliet

In Shakespeare's time, children, especially girls, were expected to obey their parents without question. What do you learn from the extract about the attitude of Juliet's parents towards their daughter and of Juliet's behaviour towards them? In your answer you should write about:

- what Lord Capulet says and does: in particular, the language he uses towards Juliet – what, for example, is suggested by his use of words like 'whining mammet' and 'Graze where you will'?

- what Lady Capulet says and does: in particular, her response to Juliet at the end of the scene
- what Juliet says and does: in particular, consider the situation she is in at the start of the scene and how she behaves towards both her parents.

Now read carefully this extract from 'The Young Couple' by Ruth Prawer Jhabvala and then do the exercise that follows on page 62.

'The Young Couple'

Cathy, an English woman, has married Naraian, an Indian, and returned to India to live with him and his family. She finds it difficult to adjust to the culture of her husband's country and in this extract from the story we see how she unintentionally behaves in an unacceptable way.

Of course, it was not easy to do anything decisive and independent while they were living the way they were, with Naraian's family supporting them completely; and the most important step now was for Naraian to get himself a job to support the two of them. But, as they both fully agreed, it was no use rushing anything; he had to have time to look around and weigh possibilities, so that in the end he would have something beautiful and useful where he would be fully engaged. In the meanwhile, Cathy would have been glad to help out and get a job herself. She had done quite a lot of things in England, she had been a receptionist to a Harley Street specialist, a sales assistant in an airlines office. Once for a brief while a waitress in a coffee bar, but of course she realised that it was impossible to do anything like that here because of her – or rather the family's, background and social standing. The sort of jobs this background and social standing permitted her she was not qualified to do.

Nevertheless, often nowadays, after Naraian had gone out, she lay on the bed, on her stomach, one foot with a silver slipper dangling from it up in the air, her fingers twisting and untwisting the end of her golden plait, and read the Situations Vacant columns in the newspapers. It was depressing: there was nothing, nothing at all for her. It was all either for readers and senior lecturers in sociology, or for fitters and mill-inspectors preferably with experience in small-grind machines. Soon her eyes involuntarily slipped to the matrimonial columns, which amused her. But she felt frustrated.

Also, perhaps, a little bored and lonely. She met plenty of people but they were all Naraian's friends or his family, so that she began to feel almost as if they were forming a ring round her out of which she could not break. She confided this impression to Naraian, who scorned it. She was free, he insisted, to do exactly as she liked, go wherever she wanted. But where was she to go, what was there to do? She never liked to go anywhere without Naraian, and there was certainly no question of walking freely down the road: she was stared at, sometimes mocked for being white and different, certainly always an object of attention. Sometimes, when it seemed to her that she was getting a complex about this, she decided

to brave the stares and taunts and go by herself into the city bazaar. Actually, it wasn't so bad: she drew a lot of attention but she ignored it. She pretended to merge with the crowd of modestly veiled women, sick cows, pickpockets, and obtrusive hawkers. When she got home, she was breathless but quite excited. She spread her purchases on the bed with a feeling of triumph: they were invariably things she didn't need – a red velvet purse sewn over with silver spangles, green and gold sandals, a picture of a swan reflected in a lake which was made out of a piece of mirror – but she was proud and pleased with herself for having gone out to buy them.

One Sunday, at lunch with Naraian's family, she was questioned about these excursions of hers. It seemed she had been seen (one was always seen, there were so many relatives, so many acquaintances, so much time in which to pass the word around) and what had excited particular comment was that she had been alone and on foot. 'Where is the need?' said Naraian's mother, 'One word, and I shall come myself with the car to take you.' This was true: Naraian's mother, sisters, sisters-in-law, always eager to go out shopping in a car, frequently urged her to join them. But she had enjoyed herself more on her own. She looked for help to Naraian, but he was busy eating a mango; either he hadn't heard, or he didn't want to get involved. She would have welcomed a word from him to tell his family about the independence customarily enjoyed as a right by English girls.

No such word coming, Naraian's mother drove her point home further: 'Our girls don't go into these bazaars alone. It is not proper for us.'

There was a waiting pause. Cathy knew she was now expected to make a tart reply which would instigate her mother-in-law to an even tarter one, after which it would be her turn again, and so on until they had got a really good family row going. But Cathy didn't say anything. Unlike the others, she had no liking for these family rows. Instead she looked again towards Naraian, who was now busy eating the flesh round the stone of his mango, always a delicate operation calling for all one's concentration and skill. Cathy lowered her head, lifted the napkin from her lap, and folded it several times very neatly. She sensed disappointment in the air, as if she had let everyone down.

Ruth Prawer Jhabvala

Exercise 5: 'The Young Couple'

This story focuses on the clash between two cultures and their values. By referring closely to the extract, explain fully how the way in which Cathy, Naraian and Naraian's mother behave illustrates the differences between the European society in which Cathy was brought up and the one she has now moved into.

Speaking and listening

Activity

Give a talk to your class or a small group in which you describe an occasion when you felt out of place. Explain both how you got into the situation and what your feelings were about it.

Key skills

Tone and register

The words **tone** and **register** refer to the features of your writing that give it its individual quality or style. For example, your tone could be formal or informal, humorous or serious, depending on the type of piece you are writing. What is especially important is that your tone stays consistent throughout each piece of writing that you produce.

One of the key features of a writer's tone and register is the **standpoint** that the writer adopts. This means the position that you, as a writer, take up in order to convey your ideas and character to the reader. The first thing to decide is whether you are going to use the first or third person to express yourself.

If you choose to write in the first person (*I was …*) you are likely to establish an informal tone as you will be addressing the reader directly. This informality of tone is also likely to become apparent through the use of colloquial abbreviations (for example, *I don't agree with what you're saying* rather than *I do not agree with what you are saying*).

If you choose to write in the third person (*It is thought that …* or *People think …*) then your tone will become more objective and impartial as you will have removed the personal element. You are therefore likely to produce a more formal piece of writing.

Remember that if you are writing a story, then the choice of standpoint from which you relate your narrative is particularly important, as choosing the first person means that your story can deal only with events that are known to or experienced by you, the narrator. If you write a third-person narrative, you can present a more complete overview of the events in your story. Try to avoid the very common mistake of writing in the first person and then ending your story with a conclusion such as *and then I died …* which is difficult to make sound convincing!

Reading newspapers 1

Reading

Newspapers, whether we read them as hard copy or online, play an important part in all our lives. They report what is going on in the world around us and, because they are published daily and are continually being updated, we can follow key news stories almost in real time, as they happen.

The people who write for newspapers are known as **journalists** and what they write is referred to as **journalism**. Effective journalism depends on the writer's skill to convey the main points of what may be very complex issues clearly and directly to a reader who is unlikely to be in a position to spend a long time reading through densely written material. Many people read newspapers on buses and trains while they are on their way to work or glance through them at breakfast when other matters are also demanding their attention. So, it is of the greatest importance that the main points of a news article can be quickly understood – journalism is a very competitive industry and newspapers that don't deliver their news in an easily understood way are unlikely to survive for very long.

How do newspapers communicate?

> Activity
>
> In preparation for the work in this chapter, try to look at several issues of least two different daily newspapers and study the features they have in common. For example, think about the ways in which they use headlines, photographs, subheadings, columns and captions. How do these different features help to communicate the key points of the news articles clearly to a reader? Try to compare how different newspapers deal with the same piece of news. Do they show any bias in favour of or against what is being described? Does the way the articles are presented suggest that the writers are trying to appeal to and interest a particular group of readers (such as young people, older people, people with particular beliefs)?
>
> What are the main areas of news on which your different newspapers concentrate; for example, world news, local news, sports news, health features, reviews of television programmes? Once you have an understanding of the types of articles common to the newspapers you have chosen then you could consider how much space is given to each type and how wide a coverage they are given (for example, how many different sports the sport articles cover, and so on).

Here are two front-page articles from UK newspapers on an event that happened in April 2010. The first is from the *Guardian* and the second from the *Daily Mail*. Read both articles carefully and then answer the questions on page 69.

Article 1

Airports closed as volcanic ash drifts toward UK

Plume of ash from erupting Iceland volcano grounds flights across Europe, affecting tens of thousands of passengers

BY JAMES MEIKLE AND ADAM GABBATT

A plume of ash and smoke billows from the volcano in Eyjafjallajökull, Iceland

Tens of thousands of passengers across Britain and Europe were grounded today as airports closed or faced severe disruption from a plume of ash caused by a volcanic eruption in Iceland.

All non-emergency flights in the UK will be grounded from noon to six because the after-effects of the eruption have made flying too hazardous, air safety officials said.

All flights in and out of Scotland were stopped earlier today with other airports facing severe disruption until the blanket ban was announced. Denmark's air space will close later this afternoon. Airports and airlines warned cancellations and delays were likely tomorrow and possibly for longer as the ash continued to move south and east into northern Europe.

A spokesman for Nats [The National Air Traffic Service] said: 'From midday today until at least 6p.m., there will be no flights permitted in UK controlled airspace other than emergency situations.

'This has been applied in accordance with international civil aviation policy.'

||||➡

'We continue to monitor the situation with the Met [Meteorological] Office and work closely with airline customers and adjoining countries.'

A BAA spokesman said: 'Due to airspace restrictions, in accordance with international regulations as a result of the ongoing volcanic activity in Iceland, we anticipate that all flights in and out of Heathrow and Stansted airports will be suspended from 12.00 today.

'We will provide further updates as we get more information from air traffic control provider Nats.'

About 1300 flights land at and depart from Heathrow each day.

A spokesman said: 'There is going to be significant disruption, particularly in the peak periods later on.'

A spokesman for Gatwick airport said: 'We are currently still open but from midday all London airports will have no flow, no arrivals or departures.

'At the moment we have had 147 cancellations. It's a matter of safety.

'We would like to remind passengers that they need to ring their airline before setting off.'

Budget airline Ryanair said that from 9a.m., no further flights were operating to or from the UK today.

It added that cancellations and delays could also be expected tomorrow.

A spokesman at Stansted Airport said 400 to 450 flights operated to and from the airport each day and it was hard to say how many would be affected.

He said: 'Fortunately we have got past our busiest departure period.

'But this has the potential to affect flights tomorrow and beyond, depending on how long the restrictions are in place.'

Volcanic ash is drifting south-east from the volcano, located beneath the Eyjafjallajökull glacier about 120 km east of Reykjavik. About 800 residents were evacuated from the area yesterday as rivers rose by up to 3 metres.

'Volcanic ash represents a significant safety threat to aircraft,' a Nats spokesman said. 'We are monitoring the situation with the Met Office, Eurocontrol and neighbouring countries, and working closely with the airlines to help inform their decisions about their operations.'

Forecasters have warned that the ash could take days to disperse.

'The concern is that as well as the eruption, the jet stream passing through Iceland is passing in a south-easterly direction, which will bring ash to the north of Scotland and Denmark and Norway,' said Matt Dobson, a forecaster for MeteoGroup.

'But it is impossible to say how much ash will come down.'

He added: 'It could be a threat in these areas from now until tomorrow or Friday.'

The best-known incident involving the threat from volcanic ash happened in June 1982 when a British Airways 747 flight from London to Auckland encountered a plume from Mount Galunggung in Java, Indonesia. All four engines failed but the plane glided far enough out of the plume for three of them to restart and work sufficiently and allow an emergency landing at Jakarta, with 263 passengers unhurt.

Article 2

Ash wreaks havoc across Europe

Gloom … Britain, left, in satellite photo of ash

AIRLINES are today cancelling all weekend flights as the cloud of volcanic ash lingers over Britain.

Meteorologists say the ash cloud could remain over Europe for a further **FIVE DAYS**.

British Airways this morning cancelled all short-haul flights until Monday morning at the earliest.

And Thomson Airways, Ryanair and Flybe planes will remain grounded until Monday afternoon.

Air traffic chiefs said the UK will remain on lock-down until at least 7a.m. tomorrow.

But transport boss Lord Adonis last night forecast 'significant disruption' for at least the next 48 hours.

Air traffic control company Nats said the ash cloud is 'moving around and changing shape'.

Neil Morris, senior manager in the aviation team at Deloitte, said the estimated cost to

Grounded … rows of airliners stuck at Stansted yesterday

|||▶

British and Irish airlines is likely to be between £26 million and £28 million per day.

Meanwhile, BBC bosses were last night trying to find a substitute for Gary Lineker on tonight's *Match of the Day* – after he got stranded.

He was one of an estimated million Brits stranded following the flights ban in Europe.

Gary, 49, was due to jet back to Britain this morning after a holiday in Barbados.

However, it was expected he would not make it back in time for the soccer show.

Air traffic controllers had hoped flights over Britain would resume early today.

But the cloud of ash from an eruption in Iceland was taking longer than anticipated to move through British airspace and the ban was lengthened.

A number of flights from New York were diverted to Glasgow and Prestwick while restrictions to parts of Scottish airspace were temporarily suspended.

Two flights arrived at Glasgow airport this morning and passengers were taken by bus to onward destinations in Manchester and London.

Marooned ... weary travellers wait for news of trips at Stansted airport

An airport spokesman said the terminal was quiet, with only 'dozens' of hopeful passengers remaining.

The spokesman said: 'Very few people are here, in fact there are probably more BAA volunteer staff than passengers.'

Desperation to complete journeys led some passengers to ask staff for taxis to places as far away as the south of England.

The spokesman said one man yesterday took a £600 taxi journey to Gatwick.

Meanwhile fears grew that thousands of kids stuck abroad on their Easter holidays will not make it back to Britain in time for school on Monday.

Dust cloud ... cars kick up volcanic ash in eastern Iceland as boffins collect samples blown from Eyjafjallajökull eruption

All airlines are desperate to begin freeing the log-jam created by the cancellation of 35 000 UK flights since noon on Thursday.

The situation was the same across most of northern and central Europe. Planes in and out of France, Finland, Denmark, Germany, Holland, the Czech Republic and Poland were all grounded.

They were joined by Russia, Slovakia, Hungary and Switzerland as the ash cloud headed over at the pace of a slow car. However, airports in Norway and Sweden reopened.

And the British flights ban was later relaxed in Scotland. Two Boeing 757s touched down at Glasgow carrying 400 Brits from Iceland.

'Low-level' schedules operated from Blackpool to the Isle of Man, and Newquay to the Isles of Scilly. Two jets had clearance to land at Manchester.

Pretty, though ... we're promised more sunsets like this beauty over Parliament

Around 16 000 of Europe's usual 28 000 daily flights were cancelled yesterday. Aviation experts last night said the historic shut-down would cost British and Irish scheduled airlines up to £28 million a day.

The chaos began after a volcano erupted on Wednesday beneath southern Iceland's Eyjafjallajökull glacier.

It sent clouds of ash, which could clog jet engines, billowing several miles into the air.

Oasis frontman Liam Gallagher, 37, was among celebrities caught up in the havoc.

He was on holiday with his family in Florida, and livid because he could not get back for today's derby football match between Manchester City and Manchester United.

Exercise 1: Icelandic volcano

1 Article 2 was published two days after Article 1. In what ways does it provide the reader with additional information?

2 Make a list of the facts that you learn from these articles about the eruption of the Icelandic volcano and the problems that were caused for air travellers and other people.

3 Write a detailed comparison of the way these two articles present the news story. In particular you should think about:
- the tone of the headlines and the language used in the articles
- their use of photographs
- their use of quotes
- the individual people each article refers to
- the range and type of information contained in each article.

Both of these articles are typical of ways that newspapers present stories for their readers. One approach, which is used especially in Article 2, is to focus on the events from a human perspective. Here, this is done by referring to the experiences of two famous figures in sport and entertainment who were caught up in the plane delays as well as by using photographs that show ordinary people waiting at airports. Similarly, both articles include direct quotes from people representing different airlines to make the news seem more immediate.

Sports news

Most newspapers devote a considerable number of pages to reporting both local and international sporting events. Usually, sports news can be found on the back pages, which means that readers whose main interest is in sport can very quickly find the section they are looking for.

Reporting sports news, however, requires a slightly different approach to reporting international news. For example, the eruption of the Eyjafjallajökull volcano in Iceland and its effects on air travel was an event that would interest readers throughout the world because air travellers and their families from all parts of the world were affected. However, the outcome of a basketball game between, for example, teams from Canada and Chile is likely to be of interest only to readers from the two countries involved and only to people in those countries who are interested in basketball. As a result, such a match is unlikely to be reported in a newspaper published in Australia and may have only a limited report in both the Canadian and Chilean press (although, almost certainly, the angle from which the report is written will be different depending on which country's newspapers you read).

The two reports that follow on pages 71–74 both describe events at the Commonwealth Games held in New Delhi in India in 2010. Read the first report carefully and then answer the questions on page 72.

Jamaican sprinter Lerone Clarke strikes gold at Commonwealth Games

BY LAURA REDPATH

Senior *Gleaner* Writer

HIS FRAME was small, he had a determined spirit and was as fast as lightning.

He represented Jamaica and was placed first in the 100m race.

'I'm not talking about the lightning bolt, I'm referring to this one, you know, Seabiscuit,' said Pablo McNeil, former William Knibb High School coach.

Champion sprinter Lerone 'Seabiscuit' Clarke can now add the Commonwealth Games to his growing list of accomplishments.

Seabiscuit was born undersized and grew to become a champion thoroughbred horse during the Great Depression, and a symbol of hope for many Americans.

'Clarke's determination and anatomical structure made me name him Seabiscuit,' McNeil said with a chuckle.

McNeil, who once sprinted for Jamaica, also coached Usain Bolt (the 'lightning bolt') when the star sprinter attended William Knibb High.

'What Lerone has done supersedes my humility,' McNeil said, his voice cracking with admiration. 'I am very happy for him.'

Ephrain Clarke, father of Lerone, said he sent up quite a few prayers on his son's behalf.

'I pray last night [Wednesday]. I said another one this morning and another one five minutes before the race.

'Then I heard the news on the radio and tears just come from my eyes.'

Ephrain said he felt a great deal of pride, considering Lerone's track and field struggles.

Jamaica's Lerone Clarke celebrates as he wins gold in the men's 100 m final during the Commonwealth Games at the Jawaharlal Nehru Stadium in New Delhi, India, yesterday

'I was saying to [Lerone] that he better put down track and field and go get a good job.

'But he said, "No, that me love, Daddy, that me love." That man teach me something.'

Perseverance

The lesson learned was perseverance, which Lerone's current coach, Vincent Thomas, said the athlete has much of.

'It has been hard to survive in this field. When you don't have the contract, it's very difficult to make it. Up to 2009, he was working at Coles Department Store,' said Thomas, who coaches at Lincoln University in Pennsylvania.

'He was coming to practise when he could, but it was tough to work six to eight hours,' Thomas added.

||||➡

Thomas said he has shouted repeatedly at Lerone, telling him to quit track and field if he could not handle it, or to choose track and field and stick to it.

Lerone left his job and dedicated his time to training, spending most of his time at the track by himself.

'He is the Commonwealth champion. He's the 2010 champion and no one can take that from him. It is the reward for the hard work he has put in.

'A lot of people would have quit already,' Thomas said.

Exercise 2: Lerone Clarke

1 Explain, using your own words, why Lerone Clarke was given the nickname 'Seabiscuit'.
2 Which other famous sprinter attended the same school as Lerone Clarke?
3 Who is Lerone Clarke's current athletics coach?
4 Explain Pablo McNeil's comment that what Lerone has done 'supersedes my humility'.
5 From information contained in the report, explain as fully as you can what you have learnt about Lerone's early life and the relationship between him and his father.

Now read carefully the report on pages 73–74 and then answer the questions that follow on page 74.

Commonwealth Games/Diving:
Magnificent Pandelela

Pandelela Rinong proudly shows the gold medal she won in the 10 m platform yesterday

THE Negaraku was played for the first time ever at a Commonwealth Games aquatics venue yesterday and Malaysia had the impish Pandelela Rinong to thank.

The 16-year-old, who has shown so much promise, proved that the faith in her was justified with a magnificent win in the 10 m platform, a result which pushed the world-class Australians into second and third place.

It was also the end of the bridesmaid's tag for Pandelela, who had won two silvers in the inaugural Youth Olympics in Singapore and in the Commonwealth Games, and was runner-up with Leong Mun Yee in the 10 m platform synchro on Sunday.

Her gold was delivered in stunning style as Pandelela had to produce a superb dive to pip Australian Melissa Wu to the gold and that is exactly what she did.

'I dedicate this gold medal to my parents for the support they have given me,' said Pandelela.

It was a triumph which had not looked possible after her second dive, which gave her a mere 58.05 points after opening with a 79.50.

If her first dive had given her a four-point lead over Melissa, the second saw her dropping to fourth.

'I felt a little frustrated as after my first dive, I thought I had a chance of winning gold but the second dive kind of spoilt it.'

But Pandelela displayed maturity beyond her years as she pulled herself together.

'I told myself to just focus on my remaining dives as I still had a chance for a medal finish and that was very important.'

She also kept reminding herself that she had beaten the Australian in last year's world championships, where Pandelela finished fifth and Melissa sixth.

That saw her edging closer and closer to Melissa and when Pandelela, who was the last to dive by virtue of finishing qualifying as the top ranked diver, made her way to the platform, her coach's advice was ringing in her ears.

'He told me to think only of a perfect dive and nothing else. The Australian was still in the lead but if I executed my final dive perfectly, the gold would be mine.'

Which she did and the judges rewarded her with 81.60, the highest scoring dive of the night, and gold was won by the slimmest of margins as Pandelela's final score was 371.05 while Melissa had 369.50. Bronze was won by another Australian, Alexandra Croak.

Malaysia's challenge in the men's 3 m springboard ended with Yeoh Ken Nee the best finisher in sixth place with 422.30 points. Bryan Nickson Lomas was seventh (419.30) while Muhd Fakhrul Md Zain (381.50) was tenth.

That didn't matter though and as Pandelela took her medal march, the impish smile was firmly on her face and her thoughts were with her parents but she had done the whole of Malaysia proud.

Exercise 3: Pandelela Rinong

1 What is the name of Malaysia's national anthem?
2 Explain, using your own words, what is meant by the statement, 'It was also the end of the bridesmaid's tag for Pandelela'.
3 Why was Pandelela the last person to dive in the competition?
4 What was the advice of Pandelela's coach that helped her to win the gold medal?
5 Using your own words, give details of all that you have learnt about Pandelela's career as a diver before she won the gold medal at the Commonwealth Games.

Exercise 4: Comparing sports reports

The two sports reports you have read are from the national newspapers of the two athletes' home countries (the *Daily Gleaner* of Jamaica and the *New Straits Times* of Malaysia). What similarities and differences can you find in the way the journalists:

1 describe and give details about the two athletes
2 write about the relationships between the athletes and their parents and between the athletes and their coaches
3 describe the competitions in which the two athletes won their gold medals
4 write about the athletes' earlier careers
5 include features (such as quotations and local details) which are aimed at readers in the athletes' home countries.

Newspaper language and other features

Headlines

One of the key features of newspapers is their use of **headlines**. These appear at the head of an article, are usually in bold and in a larger font size than the article that they introduce. It is also likely that the article itself will be broken up by **subheadings** which highlight main points in a particular section of the article.

The important point about headlines is that they should immediately grab the readers' attention in order to attract them to read the article which follows. However, most newspaper headlines do not reveal full details of the story: for one thing there is not enough space to do so and for another there would be no point in reading the whole article if all the details could be obtained from the headline. So, headline writers take a rather adventurous approach to the language they use to attract readers. Most headlines use short words whenever possible – among the most common are *deal, cost, ban, hit, clash* – and frequently use a combination of two nouns – *Petrol cost soars* rather than *The cost of petrol is rising*.

Another feature of headline language is the use of the simple present tense of verbs – *Inflation hits highest peak* – and the use of the infinitive form of the verb to express the future – *President to call election in summer*.

Headlines frequently use inverted commas to show that a detail or event is quoted or reported – *Pop group to do 'no more live gigs'*. As a result of aiming to be as brief as possible, they can on occasions produce amusing ambiguities (quite possibly intentional): *Kids make healthy snacks* introduced an article about what was being taught in Home Economics cookery lessons, not one about cannibalism!

As you will have noticed, the effect of such language is to produce a punchy and eye-catching statement which uses vocabulary (such as *clash*) that is clearly intended to emphasise the dramatic nature of the news being reported.

Language within news articles

There are also particular language features that are frequently used within news articles. Journalists are not always fully sure of the facts of the story that they are reporting and so, in order to avoid legal repercussions, they make great use of phrases such as *It is believed that …, It is feared that …, It is claimed that …, He alleges that …* . Another feature of newspaper language, used to make the writing shorter and punchier, is the stringing together of adjectives and nouns: *Cash cut-back threat*; *Key roles swapped by United forwards*.

Human interest

One of the most important features of newspaper reports is the 'human interest' angle. In order to bring their stories to life and to appeal to the interests of their readers, journalists often include personal details about the people in their stories, even if they have no direct relevance to the events being reported. For example:

> The accident was witnessed by a 17-year-old blonde youth wearing blue jeans and a red sweatshirt. The victim, Andrea Lee, 55, was taken to hospital but later discharged and returned to her 500 000 dollar house in the country.

Photographs

One final, important feature of newspaper reports is, of course, their use of photographs. When looking at newspapers, take careful note of how photographs are used to support the articles. Some are simply there to clarify the words of the account; others may be used more subtly. For example, a large photograph may well be there to place particular emphasis on an aspect of the report to which the journalist wants to draw the readers' attention. Similarly, if the report is critical of a certain political figure whom the newspaper does not support, it is likely that an unflattering photograph of the politician will be used.

Writing

Activities

1 Find an example of a newspaper report written in the style of language described on page 75. Rewrite the report using standard English and then write a comparison of your version with the original. For example, which version uses more words? How easy did you find it to make the meaning of the original clear?

2 The reports in some newspapers are written in a more formal style than those in the more popular papers. Look at examples of each type of report and then write two versions of a minor incident that happened at school imitating the style of each type of report.

Speaking and listening

Activity

Find a report in a local newspaper of an event at which you were present (for example, a sporting fixture, or a public meeting) and give a talk to your class commenting on how much the report differs from your own experience of the event.

Reading for pleasure

The power of the press

In November 1854, during the Crimean War, the British army suffered one of its most infamous military defeats when at the Battle of Sebastopol a small force of cavalry (the Light Brigade) were erroneously given orders to charge a large battery of Russian field guns. This event was one of the earliest battles to be reported by a war correspondent. An extract from the report by the correspondent, William Howard Russell, for the London *Times* is printed below. It inspired the poet Alfred Tennyson to write 'The Charge of the Light Brigade', which you will find on pages 78–79.

Read the report and poem carefully. You might like to think about how far Tennyson's poem reflects the details of Russell's report.

At 11:00 our Light Cavalry Brigade rushed to the front ... The Russians opened on them with guns from the redoubts on the right, with volleys of musketry and rifles.

They swept proudly past, glittering in the morning sun in all the pride and splendour of war. We could hardly believe the evidence of our senses. Surely that handful of men were not going to charge an army in position? Alas! It was but too true – their desperate valour knew no bounds, and far indeed was it removed from its so-called better part – discretion. They advanced in two lines, quickening the pace as they closed towards the enemy. A more fearful spectacle was never witnessed than by those who, without the power to aid, beheld their heroic countrymen rushing to the arms of sudden death. At the distance of 1200 yards the whole line of the enemy belched forth, from thirty iron mouths, a flood of smoke and flame through which hissed the deadly balls. Their flight was marked by instant gaps in our ranks, the dead men and horses, by steeds flying wounded or riderless across the plain. The first line was broken – it was joined by the second, they never halted or checked their speed an instant. With diminished ranks, thinned by those thirty guns, which the Russians had laid with the most deadly accuracy, with a halo of flashing steel above their heads, and with a cheer which was many a noble fellow's death cry, they flew into the smoke of the batteries; but ere they were lost from view, the plain was strewed with their bodies and with the carcasses of horses. They were exposed to an oblique fire from the batteries on the hills on both sides, as well as to a direct fire of musketry.

Through the clouds of smoke we could see their sabres flashing as they rode up to the guns and dashed between them, cutting down the gunners as they stood. The blaze of their steel, like an officer standing near me said, 'was like the turn of a shoal of mackerel.' We saw them riding through the guns, as I have said; to our delight, we saw them returning, after breaking through a column of Russian infantry and scattering them like chaff, when the flank fire of the battery on the hill swept them down, scattered and broken as they were. Wounded men and dismounted troopers flying towards us told the sad tale – demigods could not have done what they had failed to do. At the very moment when they were about to retreat, a regiment of lancers was hurled upon their flank. Colonel Shewell, of the 8th Hussars, saw the danger and rode his men straight at them, cutting his way through with fearful loss. The other regiments turned and engaged in a desperate encounter. With courage too great almost for credence, they were breaking their way through the columns which enveloped them, where there took place an act of atrocity without parallel in modern warfare of civilised nations. The Russian gunners, when the storm of cavalry passed, returned to their guns. They saw their own cavalry mingled with the troopers who had just ridden over them, and to the eternal disgrace of the Russian name, the miscreants poured a murderous volley of grape and canister on the mass of struggling men and horses, mingling friend and foe in one common ruin. It was as much as our Heavy Cavalry Brigade could do to cover the retreat of the miserable remnants of that band of heroes as they returned to the place they had so lately quitted in all the pride of life.

At 11:35 not a British soldier, except the dead and dying, was left in front of those bloody Muscovite guns ...

'The Charge of the Light Brigade'

Half a league, half a league,
    Half a league onward,
All in the valley of Death
    Rode the six hundred.
'Forward, the Light Brigade!
Charge for the guns' he said:
Into the valley of Death
    Rode the six hundred.

'Forward, the Light Brigade!'
Was there a man dismay'd?
Not tho' the soldiers knew
    Some one had blunder'd:
Theirs not to make reply,
Theirs not to reason why,
Theirs but to do and die:
Into the valley of Death
    Rode the six hundred.

Cannon to right of them,
Cannon to left of them,
Cannon in front of them
    Volley'd and thunder'd;
Storm'd at with shot and shell,
Boldly they rode and well,
Into the jaws of Death,
Into the mouth of Hell
    Rode the six hundred.

Flash'd all their sabres bare,
Flash'd as they turned in air
Sabring the gunners there,
Charging an army while
    All the world wonder'd:
Plunged in the battery-smoke
Right thro' the line they broke;
Cossack and Russian
Reel'd from the sabre-stroke
Shatter'd and sunder'd.
Then they rode back, but not
    Not the six hundred.

Cannon to right of them,
Cannon to left of them,
Cannon behind them
    Volley'd and thunder'd;
Storm'd at with shot and shell,
While horse and hero fell,
They that had fought so well
Came thro' the jaws of Death,
Back from the mouth of Hell,
All that was left of them,
    Left of six hundred.

When can their glory fade?
O the wild charge they made!
    All the world wonder'd.
Honour the charge they made!
Honour the Light Brigade,
    Noble six hundred!
                    Alfred Tennyson

In Chapter 5 we looked at the ways in which newspapers present international news events and also how they report sporting events. In this chapter we are going to consider other features of newspapers, including opinion columns and reviews.

Reading

Opinion columns

One of the main features of all newspapers are regular articles or columns written by named journalists on topics of general interest that may (or may not) be in the news that week. These columns are often written deliberately to provoke controversy, with writers taking the opportunity to express their own views or prejudices in order to cause a reaction among their readers.

Here is an example. Read the article carefully and then answer the questions on pages 82–83.

Why I hate squirrels!

A Staffordshire man has been fined £1547 for drowning a squirrel who persistently ate from his bird feeder. Quentin Letts is not impressed.

BY QUENTIN LETTS

Our seven-year-old daughter, Honor, learned about squirrels the sharp way last month. She spotted a grey squirrel in a nearby garden.

Honor was on her way to see her little friend, Mia, at the time and was in one of those chirrupy, hello-clouds-hello-trees sort of moods. Hello squirrel.

She bent down to stroke the thing. It bit her. With a hiss and a swipe of claw and a baring of fang, the squirrel had a go at Honor and drew blood from her right thumb.

Cue waterworks and wailing and, thank goodness, a shattering of our child's Disneyfied notions of an anthropomorphised animal kingdom where every little furry thing has a name and a benign character.

Honor has discovered that those little grey things in the garden are wild pests – vicious tree rats, I called them in a burst of parental anger as I examined her bleeding hand.

Grey squirrels are certainly not cutesy toys with the sort of feminised American accents and Tufty outfits you so often find on children's television.

Someone needs to teach the same lesson to those prize 21st-century twerps at the RSPCA.

Forty years ago, the Royal Society for the Prevention of Cruelty to Animals was a much-needed voice of mercy on animal matters.

It identified serious lapses of humanity towards helpless beasts and campaigned for an end to practices which discredited us as a civilisation.

The mistreatment of pit ponies [*pit* means 'coal mine'], the conditions in which livestock were taken to market, the keeping of trophy animals in tiny cages in zoos: these were issues on which the RSPCA and other animal welfare campaigners put a stop to shameful neglect.

I used to be a youth member and still remember the RSPCA's magazine, *Animal Ways*, with its black and white photos of inspectors in peaked caps and factual stories about animal husbandry. There was a brisk, slightly manly practicality to the RSPCA in those days.

Today, sadly, it seems to be losing touch with common sense and is pursuing animal rights with a furious logic that seems to have more to do with vexatious litigiousness and a big-sister view of social engineering rather than balanced, public interest charity work.

Yesterday came news of a court case which suggests that modern Britain has fallen prey to this soppy-mindedness.

The stupid thing is that it will only bring real animal welfare into disrepute.

It is the sort of idiocy, I suggest, that springs from animal 'rights' becoming a vehicle for shrill, politically minded, urban activists – often with nose studs and purple hairdos and a problem with tolerance.

A Staffordshire man was left with a six-month conditional discharge and court costs of £1547 after being prosecuted for killing a squirrel. Unbelievable but true.

All he did was kill a verminous pest. He has now had to pay a small fortune for his trouble.

Rightly or wrongly, the man was irked by the squirrel taking food from his bird feeder. He trapped the animal and drowned it (a matter of a few seconds and far less cruel than poisoning or snaring).

Some neighbour, apparently upset by his action, squealed to the RSPCA. The charity duly encouraged the authorities to take the man to court.

He was prosecuted under the 2006 Animal Welfare Act and found guilty. Talk about taking a sledgehammer to crack a squirrel's nut.

Perhaps the rot set in with Beatrix Potter. She, in 1903, produced *The Tale Of Squirrel Nutkin*, about a red squirrel called Nutkin and his brother Twinkleberry.

Potter's tale was not entirely wet. Nutkin nearly lost his life to an owl. The fact that he was a red squirrel – so much prettier than the scruffy greys which were imported from America and duly drove the reds to the margins of our countryside – was an extenuating circumstance.

But the nursery 'sweetification' of the squirrel had begun. Ooh look, little baby squirrel! At which sight, the modern adult assumes the voice of a soapy nursery-school teacher and says 'aaah'.

So it is that a century later we live with this kind of faux sentimentality which regards animals and birds such as squirrels, foxes, pigeons and crows as somehow our 'friends', as though life were one big episode of *Watership Down* [a book about the heroic adventures of a group of rabbits, also made into an animated film].

||||➡

Count me out. Squirrels are a destructive menace. They wreck saplings and take birds' eggs. The decline of the nightingale and song thrush can probably be attributed in part to squirrels.

These creatures are not innocent vegetarians, nibbling away at the grass. They are more likely to be found digging holes in your lawn while eyeing up the nearest tit's nest.

The time has surely come that we realise the damage being done to our society by the babyish caricature of wild animals as breathing cuddly toys.

They are creatures, wild in tooth and claw, and must be treated as such.

Daily Mail

Exercise 1: 'Why I hate squirrels!'

1 Why did Honor want to stroke the squirrel?
2 Put the following into your own words:
   a shattering of our child's Disneyfied notions of an anthropomorphised animal kingdom where every little furry thing has a name and a benign character.
3 Explain fully what the writer's opinion of squirrels is.
4 Explain fully using your own words:
   a) the writer's comments about the RSPCA forty years ago
   b) his opinion of the RSPCA as it is now.
5 Explain, using your own words, what the author means by 'animal husbandry' and 'vexatious litigiousness'.
6 According to the writer, Beatrix Potter's book *The Tale of Squirrel Nutkin* can be blamed for our present-day attitude of 'faux sentimentality' towards the animal world. Explain as fully as you can what he means by this phrase and his reasons for saying this.

Throughout his article 'Why I hate squirrels!', Quentin Letts uses emotive language to present a controversial point of view in order to provoke his readers. For example, he describes the result of the court case against the man who drowned a squirrel as 'taking a sledgehammer to crack a squirrel's nut', which through the use of a pun and deliberate overstatement attempts to ridicule the court's decision.

One of the animal characters in the animated film of *Watership Down*

Exercise 2: Looking at language

Re-read the article carefully and then comment as fully as you can on how Quentin Letts suggests his attitude towards the following through the language he uses:

- Honor, his daughter, and her behaviour
- the squirrel that attacked her and squirrels in general
- the RSPCA and animal-rights supporters.

Writing

A chance to respond

Activity

Not everyone would agree with Quentin Letts's views (and he almost certainly wouldn't expect them to!). Write your own opinion column in which you present an opposite view towards wild animals to that taken by this writer. Use emotive language to try to persuade your readers to share your point of view.

Reading

Reviews

Another regular feature of most newspapers are reviews of such things as new films, recently published books, theatre and concert performances and the previous night's television programmes.

The three reviews that follow on pages 84–86 are of the animated film *Toy Story 3*, and are taken from newspapers in different parts of the world. Read these three reviews carefully and then answer the question on page 87. 'Franchise' refers to the business agreement that allows Pixar to produce the *Toy Story* films.

Review 1

Lightyears ahead

BY ALEX ZANE

Toy Story 3
(U) 108 min

Pixar, the studio that started the computer animation revolution, return to the franchise that began it all.

And *Toy Story 3* shows why they remain the masters of the genre.

This is an almost flawless example of a movie that will keep pretty much any person of any age enthralled and entertained.

It's 15 years since the original *Toy Story* and the audience that first embraced Woody the cowboy (Tom Hanks), Buzz Lightyear (Tim Allen) and the rest of the gang so warmly has grown up a lot.

But fear not. Pixar, as usual, are one step ahead and have created a film that deals with adult themes such as unemployment, retirement and even the purpose of existence.

Yet it still appeals to the youngsters with a classic battle of good versus evil.

Opening with an explosive sequence that outdoes any of the summer's action offerings – bridges detonate, trains plummet and monkeys attack – we suddenly find ourselves at the point where the toys' owner Andy (John Morris) is a teenager heading off to college.

Worrying about their future and whether they'll be thrown away or sent to live out their lives in the attic, the toys decide to band together and face their fate.

That's apart from the plastic military men, who rightly observe, as they parachute out of the window, that 'when the trash bags come out, us army guys are the first to go'.

Friends reunited ... the gang are back but fighting for survival

An unfortunate mistake sees the other toys donated to a local day-care centre which, although on the surface seems a wonderful new home, turns out to harbour some dark secrets, as well as this film's major new cast members.

The best of this bunch is Ken (Michael Keaton), who, alongside Barbie (Jodie Benson), brings the exact voice to their decades-long relationship – the one we've always imagined they've had but could never actually hear.

There's also Big Baby, a child's doll who will surely set back sales of plastic infants by thousands.

The tear-inducing finale – I challenge you not to at least well up [eyes fill with tears] – is a superb and emotional end to a series that will continue to be watched and adored by new generations for years to come.

VERDICT: Five out of five

Sun

Review 2

Toy Story 3

BY PETER TRAVERS

Toy Story 3 Tom Hanks, Tim Allen
Directed by Lee Unkrich

The first two films in Pixar's animated *Toy Story* franchise are brilliant bookends, models of technique warmed by humour and imagination. *Toy Story 3*, coming 11 years after the last one, should have been a let-down. I mean, how hard can you squeeze a golden goose before the bird calls a work stoppage?

No worries. *Toy Story 3*, decked out in nifty, non-showy 3-D, is a joy to behold. It hits every button from laughter to tears and lifts you up on waves of visual dazzlement. And you don't need to take a kid along to appreciate it. After all, people, we were all kids once. And the way the Pixar wizards recreate a sense of childhood wonder is pretty near genius.

Cowboy Woody (again voiced by Tom Hanks with just the right blend of wit and hard-won wisdom) and astronaut Buzz Lightyear (Tim Allen in playfully scrappy vocal form) are toys in crisis. Andy, the boy who gave these toys a home, is off to college. He's outgrown his playthings, including cowgirl Jessie (Joan Cusack), Hamm (John Ratzenberger), Rex (Wallace Shawn), Barbie (Jodi Benson) and the Potatoheads (Don Rickles and Estelle Harris). Andy plans to put his toys in the attic. Instead, they end up in trash bags and mistakenly kicked to the kerb to await the garbage truck. Yikes! Kids and adults with abandonment issues (you know who you are) might want to give this chapter a pass.

OK, take a breath. The toys make it to the Sunnyside Day Care Center, where they meet new toys, such as bizarro Big Baby, ditzy [scatter-brained] triceratops Trixie (Kristen Schaal) and Shakespeare-spouting hedgehog Mr Pricklepants (a plummy Timothy Dalton). And Barbie finally hooks up with Ken, hilariously voiced by Michael Keaton.

The prospect of being played with by new kids delights Andy's toys. That is, until Lotso (Ned Beatty), a plush bear with ulterior motives, puts them in a roomful of hyperactive, toy-bashing tots. That scene is scary-funny. A later scene, in which the toys narrowly escape incineration, is just scary.

The fun returns in the nick of time. It's impossible not to giggle when Buzz gets his language button switched to Spanish. Still, there's no denying that *Toy Story 3*, vividly directed by Lee Unkrich from a richly detailed script by Michael Arndt (*Little Miss Sunshine*), goes darker and emotionally deeper than its predecessors. The sequence in which Andy introduces his toys to a shy little girl named Bonnie (Emily Hahn) is a heartbreaker. So is the movie. Tag it as one of the year's best.

Rolling Stone

Review 3

Bored game

Toy Story 3 fools fans to think they can accept this drivel

BY ARMOND WHITE

Toy Story 3
Directed by Lee Unkrich
Runtime: 103 min

Toy Story 3 is so besotted with brand names and product-placement that it stops being about the innocent pleasures of imagination – the usefulness of toys – and strictly celebrates consumerism.

I feel like a 6-year-old having to report how in *Toy Story 3* two dolls – Sheriff Woody (Tom Hanks) and Buzz Lightyear (Tim Allen) – try to save a toy box of childhood playthings from either disuse or imprisonment as donations to a day-care centre because their human owner, 17-year-old Andy, packs them up as he heads off to college. The toys wage battle with the day-care centre's cynical veteran cast-offs: Hamm the Piggy Bank pig, Lotso Hugs and Big Baby. But none of these digital-cartoon characters reflect human experience; it's essentially a bored game that only the brainwashed will buy into. Besides, *Transformers 2* already explored the same plot to greater thrill and opulence.

While *Toy Story 3*'s various hazards and cliffhangers evidence more creativity than typical Pixar products (an inferno scene was promising and Lotso Hugs cannily [cleverly] evokes mundane insensitivity), I admit to simply not digging [appreciating] the toys-come-to-life fantasy (I don't babysit children, so I don't have to) nor their inevitable repetition of narrative formula: the gang of animated, talking objects journey from one place to another and back – again and again.

When *Toy Story 3* emulates the suspense of prison-break and horror films, it becomes fitfully amusing (more than can be said for *Wall-E* or *Up*) but this humour depends on recognition of worn-out toys which is no different from those lousy *Shrek* gags. Only Big Baby, with one Keane eye and one lazy eye, and Mr Potato Head's deconstruction into Dali's slip-sliding surrealistic painting 'Persistence of Memory' are worthy of adult enjoyment. But these references don't meaningfully expand even when the story gets weepy. The *Toy Story* franchise isn't for children and adults, it's for non-thinking children and adults. When a movie is this formulaic, it's no longer a toy because it does all the work for you. It's a sap's [fool's] story.

New York Press

Exercise 3: Comparing Reviews 1, 2 and 3

Write a detailed comparison of the three reviews. In your comparison you should think about the following points:

- what group of readers you think the reviewers are mainly writing for
- the details each review gives you about the story of the film
- the reviewers' opinions of the main characters in the film and of the actors who voice the parts
- what the reviewers have to say about the audience for the film
- the ways in which Review 3 differs from the other two
- the overall opinions about the film expressed by the three writers – in particular think about the words the writers use to express their opinions
- whether any of the reviews would influence your wish to see the film, and why.

Don't forget that comparing the reviews means thinking about ways in which they are different as well as ways in which they are similar.

Other newspaper features

Activity

International news stories, sports news, opinion columns and reviews are just some of the regular features to be found in newspapers. This activity will help prepare you for the first group activity on page 90.

Look at a daily newspaper, perhaps one that you have at home, and see what other features you can find. For example, are there:

- local news features
- letters pages
- a leader column written by the editor
- sections on travel and holidays
- sections aimed specifically at female readers
- articles devoted to health news and information
- financial news
- cartoons and cartoon strips
- pages aimed at younger readers?

Make a list of the main features in any one newspaper for the whole of one week. Which features occur every day? Which occur only once a week? On which day?

Consider also how the newspaper uses photographs and other graphical features to support the stories and the type and size of headlines that introduce the articles.

Reading for pleasure

Keith Waterhouse, a playwright and novelist, was a prolific newspaper columnist. Here is one of his flights of fancy. It was written shortly after a general election in the UK, which explains the references in the opening paragraph.

The eggcup that does it all sideways

BY KEITH WATERHOUSE

And now for something completely trivial. Among the residual waste of last week's lost votes, lost seats, lost hopes and lost deposits, there was a sad story in the *Daily Mail* about lost dreams.

Rather cruelly headlined 'Perfectly Pointless', it told of the top twenty – or should that have been bottom twenty? – household gadgets which, despite their manufacturers' best efforts, failed to find an audience and thus make millionaires of their inventors.

Among the devices that were never in with a chance of outsmarting sliced bread were £200 electric nail files, laser-guided scissors, foot spas, electric fluff removers, hair crimpers, face steamers, trouser presses, towel warmers and back scratchers.

While sympathising with these kitchen Marconis, these bathroom Edisons, I can only express relief that my own invention is not on the blacklist.

This is none other than the Amazing Waterhouse Horizontal Eggcup, patent applied for, copyright reserved, Keith Waterhouse has asserted his rights under the Copyright, Designs and Patents Act 1988, to be identified as the sole creator of this eggcup.

The reason it is not among those Perfectly Pointless inventions is that it is still at the planning stage.

Paradoxically, if it were already on sale, it would not be on that list at all – it would be on every breakfast table.

The idea came to me – the Eureka! moment – years ago when I was tackling a tasty brown speckled egg for my breakfast.

It was a nourishing fresh egg, boiled for the requisite three and a half minutes. I had sliced off the top with the expertise of an executioner decapitating a condemned member of the bourgeoisie[1] – I know that in the North of England we are supposed to peel bits off the shell and make an entry that way, but I have fallen into southern habits.[2]

Toast soldiers were at the ready. I sprinkled salt and pepper, mixed on the side of the plate. I dipped a soldier deep into the egg. Immediately a Vesuvius of yellow yolk splattered over my tie.

And I wondered: Why? Why? Why? I do not know how long ago the human race adopted eggs for breakfast – which came first, the chicken or the eggcup? – but you would have thought we could have got it right by now.

The egg, as at present constructed, is not a fit companion for the eggcup, whether that vehicle takes the shape of a yellow quacky duck, fluffy chicken or an item of plain porcelain kitchenware.

Their shapes are not compatible.

The eggcup is designed – no one can explain why – to accommodate the egg in a vertical position. The egg was never intended by nature to stand that way up. That is why you get yolk all over your tie.

My solution is so simple that, like the Dyson Ball vacuum cleaner, as advertised on the box[3], it is a marvel that has not been thought of before.

You do not eat your egg from the top downwards, whether cleanly sliced or with the shell broken off in bits.

You eat it from the side edgeways, which then distributes the yolk evenly, rather than in spurts like a miniature oil well, and leaves your tie unmolested.

And so we have replaced the upright boiled egg with the horizontal boiled egg. All it requires is an elongated horizontal eggcup to accommodate it.

Whether it be in the image of a quacky duck or fluffy chicken I leave to my design team.

I have yet to construct and test a prototype or to find an enterprising pottery manufacturer who will turn out the things for about a farthing a gross, and a sales manager who will flood the market with horizontal eggcups in time for next Easter.[4]

But when that day comes, expect my name to be added to the Rich List.

Daily Mail

1. A humorous reference to the use of the guillotine during the French Revolution
2. The writer is referring to the supposed difference in cultural habits between the North and South of England.
3. TV
4. The writer is deliberately using old-fashioned terms for humorous effect: a farthing used to be the smallest English coin, worth ¼ of a penny; a gross is a measurement of number, meaning 144 of a particular commodity (or 12 dozen!).

Writing

Producing your own newspaper

Group activity

As a whole class, why not produce your own newspaper, based on life in your school?

1 Organise all the students in your class as if you are in a real newspaper office. First of all, you should decide on an editorial team who will have overall control of the content of the finished newspaper. They will also be responsible for both checking the accuracy of the content of the articles and checking the final text for spelling mistakes, grammatical errors, and so on. (It would be a good idea to have your English teacher as a member of this team!)

||||➡

2 Then decide what will be the main features of your newspaper. It should certainly include:

- news features (to do with recent events in school)
- reports of school sports fixtures and other school sports news
- reviews of school functions (drama and music productions, for example, and perhaps even tongue-in-cheek reviews of popular textbooks)
- a letters page allowing people to express their opinions about matters relating to their life at school
- opinion columns
- an editorial leader column.

You might also want to include a problem page where an 'expert' gives advice on coping with everyday problems experienced by students. These are just some ideas – you may well come up with others.

3 Once you have decided on the content of the newspaper, then work in small groups, with each group responsible for producing a particular section of the newspaper.

4 Don't forget to use cartoons and photographs and, if you can, make full use of your school's ICT facilities to make your paper look as professional as possible.

Speaking and listening

Group activity

A common feature of newspapers is a problem page where a columnist answers a selection of readers' letters asking for solutions to (mainly personal) problems.

In small groups, present a forum for such problems in which individual group members ask for advice and then receive it from a panel of experts (the rest of the group). (You can make the problems as comic as you like.) This forum can either be scripted throughout or, if you are more ambitious, the questions can be scripted but the responses impromptu.

Key skills

Figures of speech

Student's Book 1 looked at similes and metaphors. Here are some more figures of speech that you are likely to come across. You may find examples of them in newspapers.

Remember that although it is useful to know the name of the terms, merely spotting them (in poems in particular) is not enough to gain good marks in an examination. What is important is to be able to explain the effects that writers achieve by using them.

Oxymoron

An **oxymoron** is a figure of speech that combines two normally contradictory terms to create a special effect. For example:

> deafening silence
> bitter sweet

Paradox

A **paradox** is similar to an oxymoron. It is a situation or statement that seems impossible because it contains two contradictory facts. For example:

> The child is father to the man.

Litotes

Litotes is the term used for a deliberate understatement which is made to give emphasis. For example:

> The headteacher was really not very popular among the students.

In other words, he/she was very unpopular.

Hyperbole

Hyperbole is deliberate exaggeration for effect and is, therefore, the opposite of litotes. For example:

> The queue for the cinema was miles and miles long.

Climax

A **climax** is a list, very often consisting of three elements, in which each element intensifies the statement made by the previous one, until the last one provides the final hammer blow. For example:

> I expect to hear the truth, the whole truth and nothing but the truth.

Anticlimax or bathos

An **anticlimax** or **bathos** is, of course, the opposite of a climax. Here the final element in a list is in sudden contrast with the others with the effect that it either trivialises the seriousness of the preceding elements or (less commonly) emphasises their seriousness. For example:

> In moments of crisis I size up the situation in a flash, set my teeth, contract my muscles, take a firm grip on myself and, without a tremor, always do the wrong thing.

George Bernard Shaw

Zeugma

Zeugma is the term for when two unlikely items are linked syntactically (e.g. as objects of the same verb). Again, this can have a trivialising effect and is often linked with bathos. For example:

> He swallowed his pride and his chewing gum.

Irony

Irony is a particularly effective literary device and is a great feature of many English novels, particularly those written in earlier times. At its simplest it is very similar to sarcasm as an ironic comment means exactly the opposite of what it appears to say. For example:

> We're having an absolutely wonderful time over here.

(In other words, we're bored out of our minds.)

However, irony can be far more subtle and effective than simple sarcasm. To end this chapter with some food for thought, here is an extract from the beginning of Charles Dickens's *Hard Times*. One of Dickens's aims in this book is to attack the nineteenth-century educational belief that all that children need to be taught are facts and practical details.

In this passage, Thomas Gradgrind, the owner of the school, and a government school inspector are questioning a class of children. Among them are Sissy Jupe (whose father is a horse trainer in a circus) and Bitzer, whose head is full of 'bits' of facts. Each is asked to define a horse. The irony of the situation is that Sissy, who has lived with horses all her life, cannot do this satisfactorily, whereas the town-dweller Bitzer's answer meets the inspector's requirements. Dickens's use of irony effectively exposes the limitations of the educational system. (The passage has been slightly edited.)

Hard Times

'Girl number twenty,' said Mr Gradgrind, squarely pointing with his square forefinger, 'I don't know that girl. Who is that girl?'

'Sissy Jupe, sir,' explained number twenty, blushing, standing up, and curtseying.

'Sissy is not a name,' said Mr Gradgrind. 'Don't call yourself Sissy. Call yourself Cecilia.'

'It's father as calls me Sissy, sir,' returned the young girl in a trembling voice, and with another curtsey.

'Then he has no business to do it,' said Mr Gradgrind. 'Tell him he mustn't. Cecilia Jupe. Let me see. What is your father?'

'He belongs to the horse-riding, if you please, sir.'

Mr Gradgrind frowned, and waved off the objectionable calling with his hand.

'We don't want to know anything about that, here. You mustn't tell us about that, here. Your father breaks horses, don't he?'

'If you please, sir, when they can get any to break, they do break horses in the ring, sir.'

'You mustn't tell us about the ring, here. Very well, then. Describe your father as a horsebreaker. He doctors sick horses, I dare say?'

'Oh yes, sir.'

'Very well, then. He is a veterinary surgeon, a farrier, and horsebreaker. Give me your definition of a horse.'

(Sissy Jupe is thrown into the greatest alarm by this demand.)

'Girl number twenty unable to define a horse!' said Mr Gradgrind, for the general behoof of all the little pitchers. 'Girl number twenty possessed of no facts, in reference to one of the commonest of animals! Some boy's definition of a horse. Bitzer, yours.' ...

'Bitzer,' said Thomas Gradgrind. 'Your definition of a horse.'

'Quadruped. Graminivorous. Forty teeth, namely twenty-four grinders, four eye-teeth, and twelve incisive. Sheds coat in the spring; in marshy countries, sheds hoofs, too. Hoofs hard, but requiring to be shod with iron. Age known by marks in mouth.' Thus (and much more) Bitzer.

'Now girl number twenty,' said Mr Gradgrind. 'You know what a horse is.'

She curtseyed again, and would have blushed deeper, if she could have blushed deeper than she had blushed all this time. Bitzer, after rapidly blinking at Thomas Gradgrind with both eyes at once, and so catching the light upon his quivering ends of lashes that they looked like the antennae of busy insects, put his knuckles to his freckled forehead, and sat down again.

The third gentleman now stepped forth. A mighty man at cutting and drying, he was; a government officer ...

'Very well,' said this gentleman, briskly smiling, and folding his arms. 'That's a horse. Now, let me ask you girls and boys, Would you paper a room with representations of horses?'

After a pause, one half of the children cried in chorus, 'Yes, sir!' Upon which the other half, seeing in the gentleman's face that Yes was wrong, cried out in chorus, 'No, sir!' – as the custom is, in these examinations.

'Of course, No. Why wouldn't you?'

A pause. One corpulent slow boy, with a wheezy manner of breathing, ventured the answer, Because he wouldn't paper a room at all, but would paint it.

'You must paper it,' said the gentleman, rather warmly.

'You must paper it,' said Thomas Gradgrind, 'whether you like it or not. Don't tell us you wouldn't paper it. What do you mean, boy?'

'I'll explain to you, then,' said the gentleman, after another and a dismal pause, 'why you wouldn't paper a room with representations of horses. Do you ever see horses walking up and down the sides of rooms in reality – in fact? Do you?'

'Yes, sir!' from one half. 'No, sir!' from the other.

'Of course no,' said the gentleman, with an indignant look at the wrong half. 'Why, then, you are not to see anywhere, what you don't see in fact; you are not to have anywhere, what you don't have in fact. What is called Taste, is only another name for Fact.' Thomas Gradgrind nodded his approbation.

'This is a new principle, a discovery, a great discovery,' said the gentleman. 'Now, I'll try you again. Suppose you were going to carpet a room. Would you use a carpet having a representation of flowers upon it?'

There being a general conviction by this time that 'No, sir!' was always the right answer to this gentleman, the chorus of NO was very strong. Only a few feeble stragglers said Yes: among them Sissy Jupe.

'Girl number twenty,' said the gentleman, smiling in the calm strength of knowledge.

Sissy blushed, and stood up.

'So you would carpet your room – or your husband's room, if you were a grown woman, and had a husband – with representations of flowers, would you?' said the gentleman. 'Why would you?'

'If you please, sir, I am very fond of flowers,' returned the girl.

'And is that why you would put tables and chairs upon them, and have people walking over them with heavy boots?'

'It wouldn't hurt them, sir. They wouldn't crush and wither, if you please, sir. They would be the pictures of what was very pretty and pleasant, and I would fancy –'

'Ay, ay, ay! But you mustn't fancy,' cried the gentleman, quite elated by coming so happily to his point. 'That's it! You are never to fancy.'

'You are not, Cecilia Jupe,' Thomas Gradgrind solemnly repeated, 'to do anything of that kind.'

'Fact, fact, fact!' said the gentleman. And 'Fact, fact, fact!' repeated Thomas Gradgrind.

Charles Dickens

Writing summaries

Reading and writing

Being able to write a confident summary is one of the key skills required by a student of English and is something that will be valuable to you not only for other subjects in the school curriculum but also in your adult, working life.

Writing summaries is a test of both your reading and writing skills. A summary requires you to read something that someone else has written and to extract and express in your own words all the information in the original passage that relates to a specific aspect of it. It is, therefore, important that you fully understand what you have read and then have the skill to rearrange the relevant content of the original to focus on the essential details. Your ultimate aim is that readers of your summary will be able to understand all the relevant details of the original article without having to read the passage themselves.

Examinations in English at all levels will contain questions that test your ability to write a summary and it will help if you practise doing so sooner rather than later. It is important to use a methodical approach which ensures that you can write detailed and focused summaries. Remember that summary writing involves careful and thorough reading of the original passage in order to understand it fully. The following suggestions should help you to develop your own approach:

1 Make sure that you are clear in your own mind exactly which aspects of the original passage you are required to include in your summary. For example, if the passage is about the tourist delights of a particular area and you are asked to summarise what the area has to offer to young teenagers, you will not be fulfilling the requirements of the task if you include lengthy details of what is on offer for retired people!

2 Read the whole passage through from beginning to end so that you can gain an overall understanding of it – this is referred to as gaining an **overview** of its contents.

3 Re-read the passage and make notes of all the points it contains that seem to be relevant to the subject of the summary. You could underline or highlight words in the passage, if you have a suitable copy (but not if it's in a school textbook!), or write down key phrases in bullet-point form.

4 When you are confident that you have found and noted all the points relating to the topic of the summary, read through your notes carefully.

5 It is likely that your summary will contain two or three paragraphs at the most. Think carefully about how to organise the points in your notes. What would be the best order? *Remember*, it is unlikely the

points in your summary will be in exactly the same order as they occurred in the original as the emphasis of the summary will be different from that in the original piece of writing.

6 Once you have ordered your notes in what you think is the most suitable way, then, at last, you can start to write them up in your own words.

7 Try to make sure that you produce a balanced summary and give equal weight to each of your main points. If you have been given a word limit, it's a good idea to count up how many points you have in your notes and divide this into the total number of words you have been told to use so that you have an idea of *roughly* how many words to allow for each point (but don't get too obsessed by this).

8 It is important (especially under examination conditions) to use your own words for your summary as this is the best way to show that you have understood what you have read. However, don't get too carried away here – it may not be possible to reword technical language (and no one will expect you to) and very often trying too hard to reword the original can distort its meaning. Remember, simply turning phrases round (from a passive to an active form, for example) counts as using your own words and reordering key points of the original in an appropriate way will also give a clear indication of how well you have understood it.

9 Once you have written your summary, read it through to check that it's clearly focused and contains appropriate points.

This may seem like a lot of preliminary work and, especially if you're sitting an examination, it's always very tempting to cut corners, but cutting corners usually results in an unfocused and unorganised summary. Remember, writing a summary is not just about the writing – there's a lot of preparatory work to do to get your summary to peak condition. Usain Bolt may take only just over 9 seconds to run

100 metres, but he has spent considerably longer preparing himself to achieve that feat! Most summaries will require you to write 150–250 words; you can write that number of words very quickly (as long as you are clear in your mind as to what you are going to write).

Some don'ts

We have looked at the things you should do in order to write an effective summary. Here are some things to avoid:

- Don't start your summary with unnecessary introductory statements such as, 'In this passage the author says …'. All you need to concentrate on is providing details relating specifically to the topic of the summary.
- Similarly, don't finish your summary with a summing-up paragraph repeating points that you have already made.
- The purpose of writing a summary is to convey clearly to your readers the points the original writer makes about a particular subject. You should not, therefore, include opinions or comments of your own about the topic, nor should you include personal anecdotes, no matter how amusing they might be.
- It is very likely that the writer of the original passage will use examples or comparisons with other topics to make clear what is being explained. When writing your summary, there is no need to include these illustrations as your main concern is with the particular point that is made.
- The original passage might contain direct speech or quotations (especially if it is a newspaper article). It is unlikely that you will need to quote this direct speech in your summary – although you might well need to include the point that is being made by the speaker.
- When you read the original passage, be careful to distinguish between the facts that it contains and the writer's opinions about the topic. Keep the purpose of the summary clearly in your mind at all times: if you are asked to provide facts about a particular topic then the writer's *opinions* about it are not relevant, but if you are asked to explain what the original writer *thinks* about the topic, then his/her opinions certainly should be included in your summary.

Here is an article about the Jamaican city of Port Royal. Read it carefully and then do the exercise that follows on page 100.

The wickedest city

Port Royal is a coastal town located in Jamaica. As one of the largest cities in the seventeenth and eighteenth centuries, in the Caribbean colonies, with excellent geographic position, the city of Port Royal had a large influence.

In 1603, King Henry IV of France gave Pierre Dugua de Mons a large parcel of land on Jamaica to establish a French colony. The first expedition of settlers arrived in 1604. They selected a site for settlement on St Croix Island and started building houses. The first winter was windy and cold. Colonists were unprepared and almost half of them died from cold and scurvy. In the spring of 1605, they selected a new site a few miles away and named it Port Royal.

There were many legal problems with a trade monopoly and the city exchanged authorities several times during the sixteenth and seventeenth centuries. However, the city itself continued to grow rapidly. In the middle of the seventeenth century, the town of Port Royal had more than 5000 inhabitants.

Between 1655 and 1680, during the war with Spain, the city of Port Royal became a famous buccaneer hideout. With its excellent strategic position, many buccaneers used Port Royal as a main base for their operations. Soon, from a peaceful city, Port Royal transformed into a criminal nest. There were hundreds of drinking dens which attracted unsavoury characters. People called Port Royal: 'the richest and wickedest city in the world'. From 1670, Port Royal's influence became even larger. The legal trade in slaves, sugar and plundered goods made the city of Port Royal the mercantile centre of the Caribbean region.

In the morning of 7 June 1692, a strong earthquake destroyed almost the entire city. In just a few minutes, 33 acres of the city disappeared beneath the sea. More than 3000 people lost their lives in this tragedy. The people called it 'God's punishment on this wicked city'. The earthquake itself was not that strong, but the city was built on a sandpit and without a proper foundation, entire streets just slipped into the sea.

After the earthquake, Kingston became the new trading centre and the most influential city of Jamaica.

There were many attempts to rebuild the city of Port Royal. However, in the end, some kind of catastrophe always occurred. In 1704, it was burned in a fire; during the eighteenth and nineteenth centuries it was hit many times by hurricanes, and in 1907, a second devastating earthquake destroyed practically the whole city.

Today, Port Royal is a small town with just over 2000 souls. It has neither political nor commercial influence. However, the Jamaican government is trying to develop this city and make a tourist attraction of it. A city with this kind of history certainly deserves that.

Exercise 1: The wickedest city

Re-read the article and then, using your own words, give details of the history of Port Royal from 1604 until 1907. You should aim to write a paragraph of 120–150 words. Remember to make notes of your main points before writing your final version.

In the following extract from his autobiography *The Life and Times of the Thunderbolt Kid*, Bill Bryson writes about a game that was popular when he was growing up in the United States in the 1950s. Read this extract carefully and then do the exercise that follows on page 101.

The Thunderbolt Kid

However, the worst toy of the decade, possibly the worst toy ever built, was electric football. Electric football was a game that all boys were compelled to accept as a Christmas present at some point in the 1950s. It consisted of a box with the usual exciting and totally misleading illustrations containing a tinny metal board, about the size of a breakfast tray, painted to look like an American football pitch. This vibrated intensely when switched on, making twenty-two little men move around in a curiously stiff and frantic fashion. It took ages to set up each play because the men were so fiddly and kept falling over, and because you argued continuously with your opponent about what formations were legal and who got to position the last man, since clearly there was an advantage in waiting till the last possible instant and then abruptly moving your running back out to the sidelines where there were no defenders to trouble him. All this always ended in bitter arguments, punctuated by reaching across and knocking over your opponent's favourite players, sometimes repeatedly, with a flicked finger.

It hardly mattered how they were set up because electric football players never went in the direction intended. In practice what happened was that half the players instantly fell over and lay twitching violently as if suffering from some extreme gastric disorder, while the others streamed off in as many different directions as there were upright players, before eventually clumping together in a corner, where they pushed against the unyielding sides like victims of a nightclub fire at a locked exit. The one exception to this was the running back who just trembled in place for five or six minutes, then slowly turned and went on an unopposed glide towards the wrong end zone until knocked over with a finger on the two-yard line by his distressed manager, occasioning more bickering. At this point you switched off the power, righted all the fallen men, and painstakingly repeated the setting-up process.

Here Bill Bryson describes his experiences humorously and in a strongly individual way. The challenge in summarising the passage is to separate facts about the game from his descriptions of it.

Exercise 2: The Thunderbolt Kid

Re-read the extract and write a summary in which you explain:
- what electric football was and how it was played
- what Bill Bryson disliked about the game.

You should use your own words and write 170–200 words.

The next article is about a visit to Christmas Island in the Indian Ocean. Read it carefully and then do the exercise that follows on page 103.

Christmas Island

When I saw three crabs climbing a tree, it was clear this was somewhere unusual. Christmas Island is a tiny Australian speck in the Indian Ocean, somewhere between Darwin and Indonesia, so named because it was discovered by Captain William Mynors on 25 December 1643.

Because it is one of the Earth's far-flung corners, it has a host of wildlife all its own, and a few oddities that make it like another planet.

The first and foremost oddity is the crabs, found nowhere else in such numbers. They are found everywhere but the beach, for they are land-dwelling and, except in the breeding season, prefer the forest to the sea.

As it happens, they are also very fond of the golf course, where players are begged not to take a pot shot at the hapless creatures, and the road, where they are not so protected, although 'crab crossings' are being constructed on some of the main routes.

There is also another kind of crab on the island, the monstrous robber crab, huge, ugly and frankly terrifying, which is a less commonly found beast owing to a small but persistent enemy – the 'crazy ants'.

The locally dubbed 'crazy ants' were carelessly imported sometime between the wars and found their perfect island with no predators. So they have indeed gone crazy. To walk through the jungle is to be permanently harassed by the little beasts trying to crawl up your legs. If you keep moving, you can just about outwit them, but stop for a few seconds to rest and admire the untouched rainforest and you will soon find yourself hopping about swearing and trying to brush off unseen insects. A walker in boots and trousers might last a little longer, but it would not take long for them to reach arms and other bare bits.

So walking in the jungle seems like a good idea but isn't. And if the ants make life in the jungle uncomfortable for a walker, pity the giant robber crabs. They appear impenetrable, with their heavy armour and terrifying pincers that can crack coconut shells, but they are no match for the crazy ant. The ants may not be able to get through the crabs' thick shell, but they crawl up the stalks of their eyes and eat them.

The local insects that feed on rainforest trees have been luckier. The ants eat the honeydew they produce and in turn protect them against local predators such as wasps, spiders and parasites.

You don't even have to go to the jungle to see rare wildlife. Queuing outside the bank, I saw a fabulous gold pink bird with a long sweeping tail plonk itself idly in the car park; this was the magnificent golden bosun, which you will find nowhere else in the world, and which along with red crabs (also to be found in the bank's car park) adorns the stamps and souvenirs of the island.

You might imagine that the island was also inhabited by angry, out-of-breath dragons – a sound of roaring and puffing comes from the cave-riddled cliffs and jets of steam spurt out of the rock like dragon's breath. The Blowholes lie in the south-west of the island. Gentle swell causes spray and heavy dragon's breath; bigger swell results in thunderous reverberations and sudden high fountains of water that drench anyone standing nearby.

The razor-sharp cliffs are as dangerous as they look. You could drop fatally down to the ocean, or trip and gash yourself on the vicious rocks. A wooden walkway prevents nasty accidents, although it is no insurance against a soaking when a big wave rolls in a couple of hundred feet below. But set against an Indian Ocean sunset, the view is worth any number of soakings.

Real monsters lurk close by. The island has only a small ledge of shallows before the seabed plummets to the deepest depths of the Java Trench. Whale sharks like to come here, especially between November and April, and divers from all over the world come, too, for the experience of swimming with these vast beasts.

But yet another of the island's monsters hides in the shallows, and this one poses a real threat. With its potentially lethal sting and perfect camouflage, the stone fish is a problem on many Indian Ocean beaches. You would be very lucky and sharp-eyed to spot it and, while it isn't out to get you, it doesn't like being trodden on, protectively sticking up poisonous spines which administer a very painful and dangerous venom. There is an antidote, which most hotels and public services have available, but your foot will swell to the size of a melon and you will be distinctly the worse for wear. The wise paddler wears shoes.

You can't have an idyllic Indian Ocean island without beaches, and Christmas Island has plenty of secluded hideaways; a car is essential to reach them as they are miles from the main road down a rough track and you still have a distance to walk once you have parked. Christmas Island is remote enough to have few visitors, so that there is a good chance you can get the best beaches to yourself. Flying Fish Cove is the most accessible because it is on the road, and even here the snorkelling is top quality and the waters crystal clear.

Exercise 3: Christmas Island

Write a summary of what the writer tells us about the wildlife of Christmas Island both on land and in the sea. You should write about 250 words. Use your own words as far as possible.

Summarising information from more than once source

Writing a summary that takes information from more than one source is a slightly more challenging task. On pages 104–106 you will find three articles about Bako National Park in Borneo. Two of these articles are mainly factual, one was written by a tourist who had visited the park. As you will see, some information is given in more than one article.

Read all three articles carefully and then do the exercise that follows on page 106.

Lonely Planet review

Sarawak's oldest national park, Bako National Park is a 27-sq-km natural sanctuary located on a jagged peninsula nestled between the mouths of the Sarawak and Bako rivers and jutting out into the South China Sea. Although it's less than 20 km from downtown Kuching as the crow flies, it feels like worlds and eons away.

At park headquarters (Telok Assam) you'll find accommodation, a cafeteria and the park office. The office is about 400 m along a wooden boardwalk from the boat dock. Staff will show you to your quarters and can answer any questions about trails. There's a large trail map hanging outside the office; ask for a free copy. Storage lockers are available for around RM5 per day.

There's a good, if slightly scruffy, information centre here, with photos and displays on various aspects of the park's ecology. An entertaining video on the proboscis monkey is shown at regular times and also on request – ask at the office.

Bako is a lovely national park only an hour's drive away from Kuching. Camp for a few nights at the basic cabins here, where you'll lie metres away from Borneo's second most famous inhabitant, the proboscis monkey. They surround the entire area and it is one of the only ways to see these strangely human-like creatures, with massively protruding noses, close-up.

Also at the park you'll see the omnipresent troupes of thieving macaque. Often coined as 'rats of the jungle', they'll eat anything, including your lunch, right out of your hands. The more docile, gentle silver leaf monkeys also dart around the trees in the mangroves where you land.

The boat can't dock right up to the beach, so you'll have to wade through knee-deep seawater to get to the shore, which is all part of the Bako adventure (there are no roads to Bako).

There are dozens of walks all across the jutting peninsula to keep you occupied during the day, and you might even stumble across a reassuring, crocodile-free beach, which makes for a nice change in the otherwise unswimmable waters of the rest of the island. After all that walking in equatorial heat, you'll appreciate a nice cool dip.

The park also offers a night walk where it is possible to see the elusive slow loris and tarsier, tiny nocturnal primates with eyes like saucers, which give their hiding spots away under the flashlight's beam. It's these very eyes which make them endangered species; people either find them cute or are superstitious about what they can see.

Bako National Park

Anyone can visit Bako National Park in a day. Located 37 kilometres from Kuching, the park is rich with plants and wild-life typical of Sarawak. Although it is one of Southeast Asia's smallest national parks, it contains almost every type of vegetation found in Borneo.

Bako is also easy to explore. Jungle trekking is the best way to experience the richness of the park's treasure. A system of sixteen walking trails allows you to choose between full-day jungle hikes or gentle strolls. The circular Lintang trail passes through all of Bako's vegetation types including forests, mangroves and delicate cliff vegetation. The Telok Delima and Telok Paku trails provide the best views of the park.

The park can only be reached by a twenty-minute boat ride from Kampung Bako. It has been protected since 1957, so the animals have become used to human visitors. This means there is a good chance of seeing wildlife and getting close enough to take photographs.

IIII➡

The proboscis monkey, only found in Borneo, may be the star attraction of the park but you can also see long-tailed macaque monkeys, usually patrolling the park headquarters, silvered leaf monkeys, monitor lizards and squirrels. Bako is also a good place for bird watching, particularly for seeing the hornbills. There are more than 150 species of birds at Bako, including some rare varieties.

Small bays, steep cliffs and sandy beaches make Bako's coastline a delight. It is advisable not to go there between the months of October to March as the sea gets rough because of the monsoon and the park may be closed. The best time to visit is during the drier season of April to September.

Exercise 4: Bako National Park

Imagine that you are part of a team organising a two-day visit to Bako National Park for your class at school. You have been asked to write a letter to parents explaining what there is to see and do at the park. You should use details from the three articles that you have read and write 300–350 words.

Reading for pleasure

So far in this chapter we have been looking at summarising texts and reducing what was written to its key points. The ability to select and edit material is an important life skill and something that you will need to practise in a wide variety of school subjects and in the world of work.

In the passage that follows, the American novelist Edith Wharton recounts a motoring tour that she made in England with her friend Henry James, another American novelist. The two writers are uncertain of their route and stop the car to ask directions of a man in the street. James spoke, as he wrote, in long, complex sentences using formal and grandiose vocabulary. The prolixity of his question is very effectively countered by the answer it receives! (If you don't know what 'prolixity' means, read the passage then have a guess before you look it up.)

Where is ...?

'My good man, if you'll be good enough to come here, please; a little nearer – so,' and as the old man came up: 'My friend, to put it to you in two words, this lady and I have just arrived here from Slough; that is to say, to be more strictly accurate, we have recently passed through Slough on our way here, having actually motored to Windsor from Rye, which was our point of departure; and the darkness having overtaken us, we should be much obliged if you would tell us where we now are in relation, say, to the High Street, which, as you of course know, leads to the Castle, after leaving on the left hand the turn down to the railway station.'

I was not surprised to have this extraordinary appeal met by silence, and a dazed expression on the old wrinkled face at the window; nor to have James go on: 'In short' (his invariable prelude to a fresh series of explanatory ramifications), 'in short, my good man, what I want to put to you in a word is this: supposing we have already (as I have reason to think we have) driven past the turn down to the railway station (which in that case, by the way, would probably not have been on our left hand, but on our right) where are we now in relation to …'

'Oh, please,' I interrupted, feeling myself utterly unable to sit through another parenthesis, 'do ask him where the King's Road is.'

'Ah –? The King's Road? Just so! Quite right! Can you, as a matter of fact, my good man, tell us where, in relation to our present position, the King's Road exactly is?'

'Ye're in it,' said the aged face at the window.

Edith Wharton

Key skills

Vocabulary

Homonyms, homophones and homographs

The Greek prefix *homo–* means 'the same'. The exercises in this section are all based on groups of words that have similarities.

- **Homonyms** are words that have the same spelling and pronunciation, but different meanings. For example, *bit* can mean a small item of something and *bit* can be the past tense of the verb 'to bite'.
- **Homophones** are words that have the same pronunciation but a different spelling and different meanings, such as *rain* (something wet that falls from the sky), *rein* (a device for controlling a horse) and *reign* (rule as king or queen).
- **Homographs** are words that have the same spelling but different pronunciations and meanings, such as *close*, a verb meaning 'shut', and *close*, an adjective meaning 'near to'.

Being able to distinguish between words in these categories is important; you need to be able to do this in order to write and speak English fluently.

Exercise: Homonyms

The following words all have at least two different meanings. Use each word in at least two different sentences which make their meanings clear:

bear bow fair lap lean lie page pen plain train

Exercise: Homophones

Use each of the following pairs of words in sentences, making clear the differences in their meanings:

allowed/aloud ascent/assent bare/bear berth/birth cereal/serial

flair/flare freeze/frieze higher/hire hoarse/horse pedal/peddle

Exercise: Homographs

The following words have a different meaning depending on how they are pronounced. Write two sentences for each word to illustrate their different meanings:

bow desert entrance lead live minute refuse row wind wound

Variations in spelling

Some English words are spelt differently depending upon what part of speech they are. Here are some examples:

Verb	Noun
advise	advice
practise	practice
prophesy	prophecy
license	licence
affect	effect

The story of English

Reading

The population of the world is about 7 billion (7 000 000 000) people. As a rough estimate, there are about 5500 different languages spoken around the globe with about 200 languages having 1 million or more speakers. The most commonly spoken language is Mandarin Chinese, which has nearly 900 million native speakers (people who have spoken the language since they were young children). English is the third most commonly spoken language in the world, with about 350 million native speakers (approximately 5 per cent of the world's population).

However, English is spoken far more widely than any other language and, particularly through the influence of the internet, is spreading significantly. Throughout the world, 52 countries (from Antigua to Zimbabwe) have English as an official language and in a further 53 countries English is widely understood by a large number of the population. The shaded areas in the map below show the countries in which English is an official language.

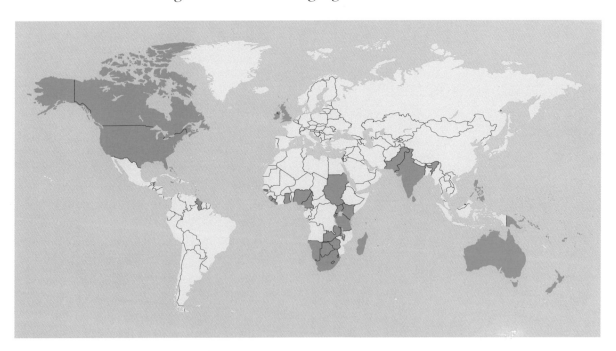

In this chapter we are going to look at the story of English – where it came from, how it developed, the different types of English spoken around the world. This will help you gain some understanding of the key features of a language that you can use to communicate with people far away from where you live.

The flowchart that follows on pages 111–115 shows how the story of English began with the Celts and how different ingredients were added over the centuries to make English the language we have today.

The original inhabitants of the British Isles were the Celts, who (not surprisingly) spoke a language called **Celtic** (pronounced *keltic*). About 2000 years ago, the Romans conquered England and established themselves as rulers there. Although they had a great influence on the infrastructure of British society, building roads and forts, for example, they rarely used the Celtic language and continued to speak **Latin** among themselves. The Celts continued to speak Celtic to each other.

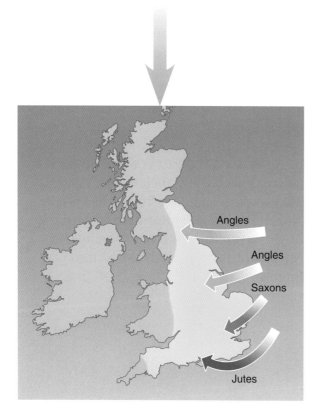

About 1500 years ago, Britain was invaded (and settled) by tribes from mainland Europe (from the area that is now Germany). These tribes were known as the Angles, Saxons and Jutes and they spoke various dialects of a **Germanic** language. When they settled in mainland Britain, they, naturally, brought their language with them.

The invading Germanic tribes drove the Celts into the wilder parts of the British Isles (in particular, the far south-west of England, Wales, Scotland and Ireland). When the Celts moved to these areas, they took their language with them. Only a very few words from Celtic survived in the areas inhabited by the Angles, Saxons and Jutes.

One Celtic word that remained in usage was 'cwm' (pronounced *koom*), which means 'valley'; it survives today in place names such as 'Ilfracombe' and 'Combe Martin' in Devon. The Western Cwm, a high valley on the approach to Everest from Nepal, was given this name by the English climber George Mallory, probably out of affection for the cwms in the Welsh mountains.

Over time, the language of the Germanic tribes became established as the main language spoken in what is now England. It is referred to as **Old English** or **Anglo-Saxon**.

Old English is an 'inflected' language. This means that the endings of nouns change to indicate which case they are (subject, object, possessive, etc.) and the endings of verbs also change depending on whether they are first, second or third person, singular or plural. Many modern languages are inflected, such as German, French and Spanish.

Many examples of written Old English still survive, such as the epic poem *Beowulf* and the historical *Anglo-Saxon Chronicle*, which was written by monks over several centuries.

During the eighth and ninth centuries, Britain was subjected to raids by people from Scandinavia (known as Vikings from the Old English word 'wicing', which meant 'pirate'). These raids were recorded in the *Anglo-Saxon Chronicle*. Eventually, it was agreed that the Vikings could establish a settlement on the east coast of England in an area called the Danelaw. The Vikings, who spoke a language known as **Old Norse**, settled and intermarried with the Anglo-Saxons and as a result many Old Norse words became absorbed into Old English.

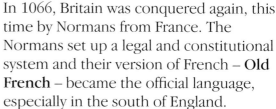

In 1066, Britain was conquered again, this time by Normans from France. The Normans set up a legal and constitutional system and their version of French – **Old French** – became the official language, especially in the south of England.

Over time, Old French and Old English combined and developed into what is now known as **Middle English**. This form of English has strong elements of French but, because of incompatibility between Old English and Old French, the inflected forms of Old English began to disappear and word order became the main way to distinguish between the different cases of nouns.

During this period, there was no one standard form of English being spoken; the language spoken by people in the North-West Midlands differed considerably from that spoken by their fellow countrymen in the south (which was closer to France and to the court, which was still ruled by French-speaking monarchs). The extracts from *Sir Gawain and the Green Knight* and Chaucer on pages 118–119 and 120 will show you an example of these differences.

In the second half of the fifteenth century, William Caxton invented the printing press. This invention meant that books, instead of being written by hand in manuscript form, could be produced in large numbers and read by a wider number of people. The result was that a more standardised version of English (that spoken in the south-east) became common throughout England.

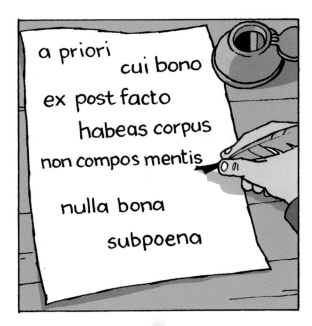

During the Renaissance period of European history (fourteenth to sixteenth centuries) there was a great revival of classical learning and Latin became the official language of legal and other formal documents in Britain. At this time a vast number of words deriving from the Latin written in ancient Rome became absorbed into the English language.

By the time of Queen Elizabeth I and William Shakespeare, the English spoken in the British Isles was similar to the English we speak today and so the period of **Modern English** had begun. The form of English which had developed was a very flexible language; Modern English not only contained a very wide vocabulary (drawn from all the different languages that had formed it) but was also able to incorporate words and usage from other languages throughout the world.

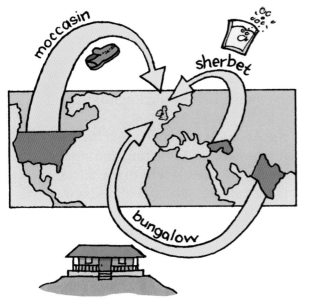

As the British Empire expanded during the eighteenth and nineteenth centuries and as trade and political agreements were established with other countries so words from those countries became part of English – for example, 'sherbet' from the Middle East, 'moccasin' from North America and 'bungalow' from the Indian subcontinent.

English is continuing to expand and develop. Each English-speaking country is developing its own unique form of the language and the ease of worldwide communication today, especially via the internet, means that all forms of English are continually influencing each other. The story of English has not yet reached its ending.

Discovering literature

The three extracts that follow on pages 116–120 are from poetry composed in English before 1400. In each case a translation or glossary is provided to help you to understand what you read. By studying these extracts you will gain some understanding of how the English language has developed.

The first extract is taken from the Anglo-Saxon epic poem *Beowulf*. The poem was composed anonymously, possibly at some time during the eighth century, but not written down until later. It tells of the adventures of the great hero Beowulf, a man of great strength, and of his battles against monsters and a dragon. This part of the story is set in the palace of Heorot, the court of Hrothgar, the King of Denmark, which is repeatedly attacked by the monster Grendel. Beowulf and his men are waiting within Heorot for Grendel to attack. This extract describes the monster making its way towards them.

Read the extract and the translation that follows it.

Beowulf

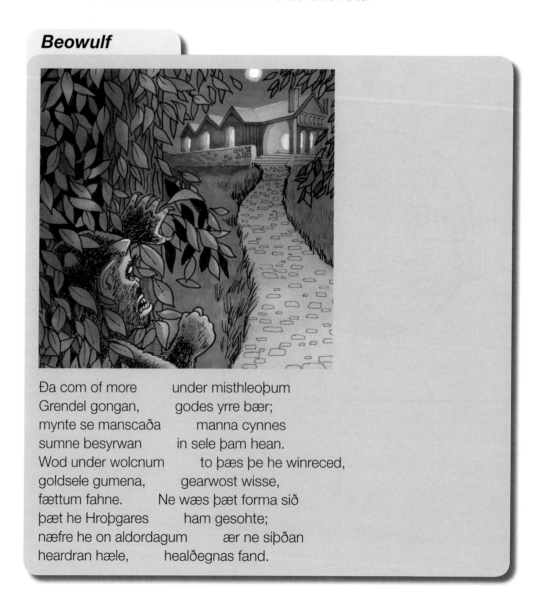

Ða com of more   under misthleoþum
Grendel gongan,   godes yrre bær;
mynte se manscaða   manna cynnes
sumne besyrwan   in sele þam hean.
Wod under wolcnum   to þæs þe he winreced,
goldsele gumena,   gearwost wisse,
fættum fahne.   Ne wæs þæt forma sið
þæt he Hroþgares   ham gesohte;
næfre he on aldordagum   ær ne siþðan
heardran hæle,   healðegnas fand.

Translation: *Beowulf*

Then, from off the moor, under the cover of darkness, came Grendel; he carried the wrath of God. He, the evil-doer, intended to ensnare some of the human beings in that high hall. Enraged beneath the heavens, he knew very well the paved road that led to the hall where men were given gifts of gold and drinks of wine. Indeed, that was not the first time that he had sought out the home of Hrothgar; however, never in earlier days (either before or since) would he find stronger heroes among the servants in the hall.

Now compare the translation with the original version. How many words can you find that are similar to their modern English equivalents? You will also notice that there are some letters in the original version that are no longer part of the English alphabet. These are:

- æ –known as 'ash' and pronounced *air*
- þ – known as 'thorn' and pronounced as the *th* sound in *thin*
- Ð/ð – known as 'eth' and pronounced as the *th* sound in *this*.

The next extract is from the anonymous fourteenth-century poem *Sir Gawain and the Green Knight*. This is a long narrative poem, set in the court of the legendary King Arthur, and tells of the strange challenge made by a knight, all green in colour and clothing, to Arthur's nephew, Sir Gawain. It is written in the North-West Midlands dialect of Middle English.

Read this extract and then compare it with the translation that follows. The symbol ȝ represents the letter known as 'yogh', which is no longer in the modern English alphabet. It is pronounced like *ch* in the German word *nicht* and is now indicated by the letters 'gh', as in 'knight' (which in Middle English would have been pronounced *kernicht*).

Sir Gawain and the Green Knight

Þe grene knyȝt vpon grounde grayþely hym dresses,
A littel lut with þe hede, þe lere he discouerez,
His longe louelych lokkez he layd ouer his croun,
Let þe naked nec to þe note schewe.
Gauan gripped to his ax, and gederes hit on hyȝt,
Þe kay fot on þe folde he before sette,
Let him doun lyȝtly lyȝt on þe naked,
Þat þe scharp of þe schalk schyndered þe bones,
And schrank þurȝ þe schyire grece, and schade hit in twynne,
Þat þe bit of þe broun stel bot on þe grounde.
Þe fayre hede fro þe halce hit to þe erþe,
Þat fele hit foyned wyth her fete, þere hit forth roled;
Þe blod brayd fro þe body, þat blykked on þe grene;
And nawþer faltered ne fel þe freke neuer þe helder,
Bot styþly he start forth vpon styf schonkes,
And runyschly he raȝt out, þere as renkkez stoden,
Laȝt to his lufly hed, and lyft hit vp sone;
And syþen boȝez to his blonk, þe brydel he cachchez,
Steppez into stelbawe and strydez alofte,
And his hede by þe here in his honde haldez;
And as sadly þe segge hym in his sadel sette
As non vnhap had hym ayled, þaȝ hedlez he were
    in stedde.
He brayde his bulk aboute,
Þat vgly bodi þat bledde;
Moni on of hym had doute,
Bi þat his resounz were redde.

For þe hede in his honde he haldez vp euen,
Toward þe derrest on þe dece he dressez þe face,
And hit lyfte vp þe yȝe-lyddez and loked ful brode,
And meled þus much with his muthe, as ȝe may now here:
'Loke, Gawan, þou be grayþe to go as þou hettez,
And layte as lelly til þou me, lude, fynde,
As þou hatz hette in þis halle, herande þise knyȝtes;
To þe grene chapel þou chose, I charge þe, to fotte
Such a dunt as þou hatz dalt – disserued þou habbez
To be ȝederly ȝolden on Nw ȝeres morn.
Þe knyȝt of þe grene chapel men knowen me mony;
Forþi me for to fynde if þou fraystez, faylez þou neuer.'

Translation: *Sir Gawain and the Green Knight*

The Green Knight elegantly prepared himself; with his head somewhat inclined he revealed his neck. He laid his lovely long locks of hair over the crown of his head allowing his bare neck to be exposed. Gawain grasped his axe and raised it on high; he set his left foot on the ground before him and let fall the axe swiftly and cleanly on the naked neck so that the sharp blade shattered through the bones and sheared through the smooth flesh, cutting it in two so that the bloodied edge of the blade bit into the ground. The handsome head fell from the shoulders on to the earth and people kicked out at it with their feet as it rolled towards them. Blood sprayed from the body and flecked on to the green. However, the great knight neither faltered nor fell but strode forth on firm legs and, right there where people stood, he purposefully reached out to the handsome head and lifted it up straightaway and turning to his mount he caught hold of the bridle, stepped into the stirrups and mounting on high, held his head by the hair in his hands. And he sat himself steadily in his saddle as if no misfortune had befallen him even though he was without his head. He heaved his body around, that fearsome, bleeding body; many people there had doubts about what was happening; he held up his head steadily in his hand and turned the face towards the noblest of those on the platform; he raised up the eyelids and looked straight ahead and said much with his mouth as you may now hear: 'Look here, Gawain; be sure to do as you have promised and, young man, search fully until you find me, as you have promised in this hall in the hearing of all these knights. I charge you to make your way to the Green Chapel as you chose, to receive such a blow as you have dealt to me – on New Year's Day you have deserved to be fully repaid. Many men know me as the Knight of the Green Chapel. You will have no difficulty in finding me if you ask. Be sure not to fail.'

The final extract is taken from one of the first major poems to be written in English: *The Canterbury Tales* by Geoffrey Chaucer (*c.* 1340–1400). *The Canterbury Tales* contains a collection of tales in verse ostensibly narrated by different members of a group of pilgrims making their way to the shrine of St Thomas à Becket in Canterbury. The Prologue to the tales consists of descriptions of the appearance and characters of the pilgrims and allows Chaucer to reveal their particular virtues and vices, providing us with a vivid picture of the people of the fourteenth century and the lives they led. Chaucer lived in the south-east corner of England, which was very much under the influence of the Norman-French court, and his language is much closer to Modern English than that of the author of *Sir Gawain and the Green Knight*, who lived at about the same time but in a different part of the country where a different dialect was spoken.

This extract from the Prologue describes the Miller, one of the more grotesque and scurrilous members of the pilgrimage. No translation is provided, but the words printed in italics are explained to the right of the poem.

'The Miller'

The Miller was a stout *carle* for the nones,	fellow
Full big he was of brawn, and eke of bones;	
That proved well, for *ov'r all where* he came,	wheresoever
At wrestling he would *bear alway the ram*	win the prize
He was short-shouldered, broad, a *thicke gnarr*,	tough, thickset man
There was no door, that he *n'old* heave off bar,	could not
Or break it at a running with his head.	
His beard as any sow or fox was red,	
And thereto broad, as though it were a spade.	
Upon the *cop* right of his nose he had	tip
A wart, and thereon stood a tuft of hairs	
Red as the bristles of a sowe's ears.	
His *nose-thirles* blacke were and wide.	nostrils
A sword and buckler bare he by his side.	
His mouth as wide was as a furnace.	
He was a *jangler*, and a *goliardais*,	joker buffoon
And that was most of sin and *harlotries*.	crude jokes
Well could he steale corn, and *tolle* thrice	charge
And yet he had a thumb of gold, pardie.	
A white coat and a blue hood weared he	
A baggepipe well could he blow and soun',	
And therewithal he brought us out of town.	

Geoffrey Chaucer

Reading for pleasure

If you have enjoyed what you have read, then you might want to investigate these three works of literature further. Various translations or modern versions are available (as books and online – ask your teacher to suggest versions to read); however, you might like to take on the challenge of trying to read some of the poetry in the original.

Standard English

In this chapter we have been looking at different forms of English through history. As English has now become an international language there are, of course, many different dialects and variations of English spoken throughout the world. However, it is important that when you are producing a piece of continuous writing in English you remember that the person reading it may well be of an older generation and living in a country far away. This does not mean that the reader will not be familiar with the attitudes of younger people or of people in different countries, but he/she may not be fully up to date with the colloquial or dialect terms that you might use as a matter of course when speaking to your own friends.

Standard English uses the accepted conventions of expression and grammar that are common to speakers and writers of English of all ages throughout the world. Many of the conventions of standard English have already been explained in this book and in *Student's Book 1*. However, using standard English does not mean that you have to write in an unnecessarily formal and overly literary style; it means simply using a form of expression that can be clearly understood by the greatest number of readers who will also be familiar with its conventions.

Key skills

Vocabulary

Prefixes

A **prefix** is a letter or group of letters attached to the beginning of a word that partly affects its meaning. If you know the meaning of a particular prefix – many of the most commonly used in English come from Latin or Greek roots – then you are in a good position to work out the meanings of other words beginning with the same prefix. Here are some of the most common prefixes found in English, along with their original meanings (be careful not to confuse the first two in the list).

ante–	before
anti–	against
circum–	around
dis–	not, opposite of
fore–	before
in–, im–, il–, ir–	not
inter–	between
pre–	before
re–	again
sub–	under
super–	above
trans–	across
un–	not

Group activity

1 Working together in groups of three or four, write down all the words you can think of beginning with each of the prefixes above.
2 When you have done this, check the meanings of the words in a dictionary. How many of them involve the meaning of the prefix? For those that don't, check to see whether they actually contain the prefix or whether they just happen to begin with the same sequence of letters.
3 Then use the dictionary to see how many more words you can find beginning with that prefix.

Language research

Here is an opportunity for you to research into the origins of some English vocabulary. The technical term for the study of the origins of words is **etymology**.

Exercise: Dictionary work

Here are six lists of words. Each list contains words that have entered the English language from different sources or roots: Celtic, French, Greek, Latin, Old English, Old Norse or miscellaneous other sources.

Draw up a table like the one below. Using a dictionary or other search tool, investigate the origins and meanings of the words in the lists and write them in your table under the correct heading. (Some words have been filled in already to start you off).

1 apple, berserk, bonanza, costume, delta, glen, manuscript, syrup, tambourine
2 academy, algebra, brogue, fog , guitar, equestrian, mustard, potato, sword
3 billiards, cairn, bungalow, civilian, fork, jungle, midnight, mohair, skirt, theory
4 albatross, anchor, coffee, daughter, elegance, khaki, punctuation, saga, slogan
5 animal, bacteria, brother, canoe, foyer, guest, crag, pyjama, shampoo
6 armada, alliance, banshee, encyclopedia, ghost, mosquito, nocturnal, outlaw, thug

	Celtic	French	Greek	Latin	Old English	Old Norse	Miscellaneous
1							
			delta				
2							
	brogue						
3							
				civilian			jungle

Index